BUILDHER

EMPOWERING WOMEN
TO BUILD & RENOVATE
THEIR DREAM HOME

BUILDHER

Smith Street Books

REBEKA MORGAN &
KRIBASHINI HANNON

CONTENTS

WHO ARE BUILDHER?

It all started only a few short years ago. While holidaying in Italy, we stole a moment to escape our families and get some Italian shopping under our belts. You could say that two matching jumpers and a leather coat later (we share quite frequently) we got to chatting, as we do.

We started discussing how lots of friends, and friends of friends, were contacting us for help and advice about their building and renovation projects. We shared stories of women who were experiencing avoidable issues with builders and design professionals, resulting in quotes coming in dramatically over budget. We realised there were several recurring themes: not knowing what to do and when; uncertainty around how to bring build prices back to budget; and navigating how to negotiate and easily resolve avoidable problems on the build.

We realised that these women had all the transferrable skills needed to manage their own renovations, but there was no roadmap to guide them. Between us, we felt angry that this was happening. We knew that we possessed this knowledge, so we decided to create a business where women could get the help they needed; a place where they could learn the building and renovation process; the ins and outs of how to make a big impact; and the tips and tricks we have learned through our years of experience managing building projects.

And so BuildHer Collective was born: an online global community of kick-ass women who can share the highs and the lows, raise each other up and learn from us and each other, and make friendships with like-minded women who are creating spaces that fill them with joy. That is what BuildHer Collective is all about.

<u>MEET REBEKA</u>

Outside of my family, building and business have always been my two loves. I've had the fabulous good fortune to incorporate both into the way I want to live, with the added bonus of being able to help people on their building journey, too!

Built form and how spaces work and feel have always fascinated me. I love understanding how the two go together, how I react and feel around them, how practical they are, what things I find visually pleasing about them and how other people perceive those same spaces. When I finished high school, I enrolled in a degree in architecture, but after a few years I realised that my real interest lay in the way buildings are constructed and come together, so I redirected my studies into construction management.

My degree in construction led to a series of jobs in the commercial building industry, starting as a quantity surveyor and then as a project manager on large-scale builds. I soon became the general manger of a commercial building company, which is where I met the fabulous Kribashini.

I met my amazing partner John while I was renovating a house; I had begged him to help me out as another trade had let me down. We had an immediate connection – he too was interested in building and had developed and subdivided a few properties. After a few months we had moved in and purchased a house together, which we renovated 'block style' and rented out in under two months!

Our home development journey started a few years later when we fell in love with a Victorian brick property and shared the same vision for renovation. We wanted to renovate a family home, spending money on architects and finishes in order to create a dream lifestyle in line with our values. Other builders thought we had overcapitalised and would need to live there for 10 years before we recovered our costs, but a year later we sold the property for $500,000 over the reserve, demonstrating that buyers truly value a well-designed home.

With this new-found confidence and a few renovations under my belt, I took the plunge and registered myself as a builder. I have always been confident in my building skills and being a woman in a male-dominated industry has never intimidated me. Soon afterwards, Kribashini and I decided to start BuildHer Collective, and I have never been happier. Every day we get to work with women to build their dream homes. It is truly rewarding work, and some of these women have become my best friends. The community we have created is truly fabulous, supporting each other and building each other up to get the best out of every build. We have worked hard to create BuildHer, but I have loved every moment.

Rebeka Xx

MEET KRIBASHINI

When people from my past meet me and find out what I do for a living, they are taken aback. I guess they always saw me as a particular type of person, perhaps a teacher or someone who works with children, and they are surprised when they hear I work in the construction industry. To them, my personality and the stereotypes associated with building and renovating just didn't fit. How wrong they are!

The thrill I have for starting, managing and completing a building project is unparalleled. To me, there is no better job, but it's one I might not have chosen if I had listened to people's own interpretation of my personality. It was something I fought against early on in my career, but I learned through good leadership that my personal values should shape my actions. So, I found my voice and management style and boy, does it work for me.

I have been surrounded by 'building' in one form or another since I was little. My family owned a glassmaking business before moving into painting and decorating, so ever since I can remember I have loved creating. As my career grew, I came to love everything about design and building, but what I love most of all is the variety that comes with my job.

When Rebeka and I started BuildHer Collective in 2017, we had a vision for what we wanted our business to be. At the time, I was still managing major commercial projects and had been on that trajectory my whole career. I was taking on bigger and bigger projects. And then I had to choose. Like all things in life, it took me time to reconcile this change. I needed time to get used to the idea of jumping off one road and on to another. I am so glad I took the leap.

The way I see it, the more we are informed about how the construction industry works, the better off we all are. When we know what we are asking for, we negotiate better and, most importantly, we create homes that not only function well, but are also beautiful, and together we raise the level of the industry as a whole.

My days at BuildHer are fun and full. We help so many women and I get a kick every time a question pops up in our members' community and a fellow BuildHer nails the answer. It makes me happy to know that they learned that from us.

If you have picked up this book and have an interest in design or construction and my journey resonates with you, don't be afraid to take the jump! You'll find your place. My hope is that building and renovating your home brings you the same deep satisfaction that finishing a project with purpose brings to me.

Kribashini Xx

WHAT IS BUILDHER COLLECTIVE?

BuildHer Collective teaches and empowers women to undertake their own building and renovation projects. Whether you're renovating for profit or building the home of your dreams, BuildHer arms you with the tools and knowledge you need to successfully bring your vision to life.

We believe that being a BuildHer is much more than simply designing and building a property. We say that because by taking control of the whole process, we are able to create homes that are designed for how we want and need to live. We are immensely proud of our BuildHers and DevelopHers. These women know they can truly make a difference to their build or renovation by understanding that the way we connect with our spaces, and the moments we experience in them, have positive impacts on our families and loved ones. Armed with this confidence, our BuildHers can make informed decisions about all aspects of their builds, whether they decide to be hands on or work with a team of professionals. By being a part of the BuildHer community, these women help each other out by sharing what they've learned, along with their experiences, both good and bad. That is how we all learn.

We designed our signature 'Build like a BuildHer' program and 'DevelopHers Masterclass' with a flow of modules and course content to guide women through the building and renovation process. We explain the important decisions you need to make every step of the way, with templates and checklists that provide structure to what can often feel like a murky process. We also pinpoint the tricky waters to navigate, while making sure solutions are applicable to individual situations.

Our course content is the culmination of what we have learned ourselves through our hundreds of renovations, from the success stories to the difficult projects that were a constant uphill battle. When we launched BuildHer Collective, we knew we had something special, but it was nail-biting – would people want it? We had a booth at the 'Home Show', a popular building and renovating event hosted in Melbourne, offering pre-booked advice sessions. We can still remember how excited we were to see people look at our program and overhear them say, 'I wish that was around when I built my home'.

We have grown so much since then! We are now involved in hundreds of BuildHer projects across the world, via our members' Facebook group and through our online fortnightly Q & A sessions. We love seeing designs and decisions come to life, and the enjoyment our BuildHers get from the experience just can't be beaten.

BUILDHER
THE BOOK

If you have picked up this book, then you are probably looking to renovate your home to live in or perhaps you want to renovate for resale or profit. Either way, you are about to embark on an exciting journey and this book is here to help you through the process.

When we set out to write this book, our intention was to make it both practical and inspiring. With so much 'content' available on the internet, we know how confusing it can be to figure out if you are on the right path. So, we decided the best thing we could do was map out a clear and logical framework using some of our favourite images from our most loved projects, which we hope you love, too.

We take you through the building and renovation process and share our tips for success. We help you navigate your values and demonstrate how they will help your decision making, vision and budget. We also discuss how to get each room just right and what your must-haves might be. We tackle those tricky finance questions and look at why things cost what they cost. Truly, building is fun – we have had some of our best times being part of the building process, and a big part of that is knowing what you are looking at and finishing a build knowing a lot more than you did going into it.

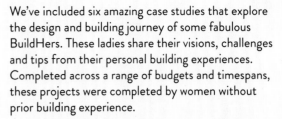

We've included six amazing case studies that explore the design and building journey of some fabulous BuildHers. These ladies share their visions, challenges and tips from their personal building experiences. Completed across a range of budgets and timespans, these projects were completed by women without prior building experience.

This book is for any woman who is thinking about renovating or building their own home or for resale. If you love all things property and have been dreaming of building or renovating for longer than you can remember, then hopefully you will find the inspiration to start among these pages. Whether you are single, a couple or have a small or large family; or you're renovating an apartment, townhouse or larger family home, this book will arm you with the knowledge you need to build or renovate successfully while enjoying the opportunity to bring your vision to life.

Throughout this book we feature some of our favourite BuildHer renovations. From left to right: Alison Lewis and her daughter in their beautiful Kew house; Ivy Huang's sophisticated and bright living room in the Armadale house; the formal lounge at Naroon Road; and the family bathroom at Cunningham Street.

GETTING
STARTED

<u>LET'S BEGIN!</u>

So, you've started to think about renovating your property. Welcome on board!

As with any project, it is important to understand the scope and scale of what you are about to embark upon, and when it comes to building we are here to help! There are many, many ways to build or renovate a home, and how you choose to approach your project, along with your level of involvement, is part of the joy. This is what will make your build unique and exciting to you; otherwise, you might as well go and buy a finished property.

We believe the building and renovation journey is one of most rewarding experiences you can undertake. It is a gift to be able to determine the space in which you want to live, the results of which will hopefully give you and your loved ones pleasure for years to come. Some of us spend months, even years, thinking about and visualising our perfect spaces, and getting started can sometimes feel like the biggest hurdle of all. That's okay! All that time and energy spent dreaming and scheming only reinforces what you ultimately want to achieve, and will help you get there in the long run.

As you dive further into your project, you will learn more about what you can and can't accomplish. There may be alternative methods or solutions to a problem that pique your interest or divert you from what you originally set out to do. You might find that you end up going round and round before making a final decision, or that you end up taking a few steps back before moving forward. Please know that this is all part of the process and the fun! We call it the BuildHer pivot. So, enjoy every hour and win along the way, whether it's looking for the perfect paint, scouring the internet for the right benchtop or building a giant moodboard of fabrics and colours. It will all be worth it in the end.

WHY DO WE BUILD OR RENOVATE?

There are many reasons to build or renovate our home, but they all start with the dream of creating a better space. This might be for aesthetic reasons, practicality, profit or a combination of all three. Sometimes we find ourselves in a home that we feel bound to and don't want to leave, even though it no longer suits our needs. This might be an emotional connection to a building's history, its location or the personal experiences we've had in that home. Other times we find that our finances are best utilised by renovating or building a property from scratch rather than moving house.

Whether we are renovating an apartment, townhouse or house, or embarking on a new build, the intention is always the same: to create the best space possible with the means available to us. Yes, there will always be limitations, and building tends to magnify these pressure points, whether it's money, space or time; but the quicker we recognise potential issues before careering down the path of renovation, the better placed we will be to address and minimise problems before they arise.

Creating the perfect home for you and your loved ones is the ultimate goal of building and renovating. The space should be a unique reflection of your values and how you want to live, what is important to you and what is not. Sometimes this is hard to achieve in an already completed home, so by planning and building or renovating your own home you are able to inject a little more of yourself and your values.

Bedrooms are the ultimate personal space. They are a sanctuary, incorporating a reflection of you and how you want to live.

The bedrooms pictured here are very different in style and aesthetic, and this is achieved by playing with space, materials and interior design. Don't be afraid to design your base and change the styling as you feel. A house should never be stagnant or stuck in a moment in time; rather it should breathe and change with you.

WHAT STOPS WOMEN RENOVATING?

Over the years, we have learned that women have an innate talent and unique set of skills to share when it comes to building and renovating. So why are so few women involved in home construction projects?

We believe that women are very much involved in their projects, but this often goes unrecognised. We work with many women who are, in fact, managing their construction works on various scales without any help or guidance, from sourcing quotes and booking in trades, to managing budgets and paperwork.

But there is often a disconnect between you, the client and the professionals employed to complete the job. At times, our vision of what we want to achieve – how our homes need to function and flow – becomes lost. This may be due to unexplained regulations, or not understanding the cost of various components, as well as the technicalities of a build. These oversights often occur because the opportunity to discuss them with the project team at key stages was missed.

Some women tend to stand back if they are not confident in their knowledge or experience of construction, and this is especially heightened in a male-dominated industry where the occasional 'man-splaining' can still inject the conversation. We believe that by learning as much as you can about the process (instead of trying to understand the inner machinations of, say, timber framing), and by holding regular open discussions with your project team, you can be confident in asserting your vision and influence the outcome of your build.

We have seen many successful builds managed by women with no prior experience in building or renovating. Once you know what to look out for and what questions to ask, have a roadmap in front of you and a willingness to compromise, everything in building is achievable.

Also bear in mind that there are many paths you can choose when it comes to your level of involvement in the project, and we are here to help you find the right one! There are some of us who prefer to work more closely with architects during the design process and then take a step back and hire a building manager for the actual build; others like to be hands on, undertaking the design themselves and coordinating the works on site; while others still like to be more involved at the back end of the project, taking on internal decorating and the selection and coordination of fixtures and fittings. At the end of the day, there is no right or wrong way to be involved. We encourage you to play to your strengths and enjoy the process as much as possible.

1. We firmly believe that all women should feel confident managing their own build and renovation projects. Don't be afraid to bring your own skills to the table – you may become building addicts like us!

2. Kitchens are one of the most intricate and technical parts of any build, and it can feel overwhelming working with so many trades simultaneously. Remember that you already intrinsically understand the needs and functionality you require, so who better placed to guide this process than you!

AN OVERVIEW OF THE BUILDING & RENOVATION PROCESS

Knowing exactly where to start can often be the biggest hurdle when taking on a potentially life-changing project. To give you a taste of what lies ahead, we have provided an overview of the process, but keep in mind that this is not always linear and you may need to take a few steps back in order to move forward, or reassess your priorities and budget as the project progresses. We will go into these in more depth a little later in the book.

Understanding the building and renovation process at the outset is key. This will help you to identify the steps that you can't manage on your own without professionals, along with other elements that you might like to take on yourself.

PLANNING

The first stage is all about planning. This is when you gather all the relevant information about your site and land to ascertain if you require planning/development approval from your local authority. If you do, this usually needs to be granted before you start knocking down walls or building. Sometimes you will need a designer to help you prepare documentation of your intentions for the application.

DESIGN

This includes all aspects of architectural and interior design work, from the floor layout, size and flow of new spaces (or the redesign of existing spaces), technical detailing and design coordination, to the choice of new fixtures and fittings including cabinetry and lighting, as well as soft furnishings and colour palettes.

QUOTING/TENDERING

Pricing your project involves obtaining fee proposals from professionals for services, or sourcing permit estimates, quotes or tenders from builders or tradespeople for labour and materials. Depending on the specific job and your level of involvement in the project, you might source rates for labour only or the cost of materials from suppliers.

PERMITS

No matter where you are in the world, building is regulated in some form or another. In most countries local councils, municipalities or authorities will need to approve the proposed 'works' prior to the project commencing. Your local area will have a criterion that determines the need for a formal building permit. If you build without one you could be liable for a fine or worse.

CONSTRUCTION

Once any required permits are approved, the job will move to construction. In its most simplistic form, this is essentially the act of combining labour, techniques and materials to create a building from a set of technical documents and specifications.

HOW LONG DOES IT TAKE TO RENOVATE?

How frustrating is it when you ask this question and the answer is: 'How long is a piece of string?' Unfortunately, we are going to say the same thing – but don't worry because there are ways to help manage your expectations and timeline for a project.

Although it may seem obvious, a good place to start is your personal calendar, as this can help determine your time requirements in relation to building and give you something to work towards. For example, imagine you decide to start renovating your home in January, but you have a three-month overseas holiday planned for September – this means you have nine months to complete the work. Depending on the scope of the renovation and the permits required, this may or may not be achievable. Now let's say you don't want to be around during construction and you want your designer to oversee the build, so everything needs to be in place by September. You can then use this date as a base for discussions with builders and tradespeople at the start of your project, to ensure they can work to your timeline. This is beneficial for all parties, as it allows the people you employ to block out dates and balance their workload.

In large-scale commercial projects, we determine the time requirements based on the needs of the business, and ask builders to price the works to meet that timeline. Of course, the timeline needs to be feasible and realistic, but the contractor will cost any time constraints into labour and resources, and forecast a construction schedule that will meet the deadline.

From the tentative first steps of looking through magazines and engaging with builders, to the design and build stage and living in the renovation, the time it takes to bring a new space to fruition can seem daunting and never-ending.

There will inevitably be good days and bad days, but don't lose sight of your vision and try to stay positive. Bad days end, and before you know it you'll be living in your new home, which you helped to create.

Top Tip

At the start of a job, agree with your professionals on how long they need to do their part of the works and make them accountable. Hold regular meetings to help everyone stay on track and always document your completion dates for each stage of the build.

Top Tip

Start gathering paperwork and information about your property as early as possible. This includes applications for loans.

At times, we see the opposite happening in the residential construction industry: the scope of the job is determined and a builder will estimate (based on their experience) how long that job will take to complete, often building in a time buffer to be safe. The size and scale of the builder's business will often dictate how much time they can allocate to preparing and scheduling a project in advance of starting.

At the end of the day, no project is exactly the same and each has its own set of unique obstacles to overcome. Other factors that can add time to your build include:

· The complexity of your site

· Obtaining specialist tests and reports

· Submitting and obtaining permits and approvals

· Objections to your build by neighbours

· Other projects your professionals may be working on

· The time it takes for you to make decisions

· The time it takes to secure finance or funding

· Lead times for materials to arrive or be fabricated

· Weather delays

· Scheduling conflicts with trades

· Building issues that might require outside involvement

· Building inspections and rework that may be required

· Poor construction scheduling and planning

· Injuries or accidents.

Top Tip
Always ask how long works or services will take to make sure they fit your timeline. Include a time buffer to account for unexpected delays.

Top Tip
If your job is large and you are hiring a building manager or contractor to manage the project, ask for a construction program or indicative milestone months for key stages of the build.

For Rebeka and John, looking at architectural plans is a part of daily life. Touching base with your build team over a morning coffee is a good way to plan the day, helping you to juggle kids and trades alike.

THE BUILDHER BLUEPRINT

YOU'VE DECIDED TO BUILD!

Go you! Let's start the journey...

1

BIG PICTURE

Start thinking about the big picture, your immediate needs and near future.

2

FUNDS

Work out how much you have to spend and how you will go about financing your renovation.

3

DESIGN

This is the fun part! Walk the streets and take pictures that inspire you. Engage a designer.

4

FINANCES

Take time to make the best decisions for you and your family.

5

PERMITS

You may or may not require a planning permit. Once resolved, a building permit will be issued.

6

TENDERING & BUDGETS

Will you hire a builder or be an owner builder? This will determine the level of tendering required.

7

DEPOSIT & SITE PREP

Understand your role during the project. Review and sign contracts, and manage your timeline.

8

DEMOLITION

Is there demolition to be done, and is it separate or included on the permit?

9

BASE STAGE

This stage includes in-ground plumbing and electrics, retentions and foundations.

10

FRAME

This is when the frame goes up. It can be exciting to see the form of the building take shape.

11

LOCK UP

Windows, external doors and the roof is installed. The property is now watertight.

12

FIXING

In this stage, your home really takes shape: your vision will come together, like a 3D jigsaw.

13

PRACTICAL COMPLETION

All the works are completed and the keys are handed over.

14

DEFECTS

Keep records of defects as you settle into your new home.

MOVE IN & ENJOY

Styling, styling, styling. Make your house a home!

CHOOSING YOUR BOOTS

At BuildHer, we encourage our community to 'choose their boots' before commencing a building project. As with design, there is more than one delivery method when it comes to building and renovation, and your desired outcomes, budget and requirements should influence the building model you select. Many people don't realise the options available to them and generally adopt a method that their friends or family have used, which may not be the best model for them based on their needs.

Your chosen delivery method will also determine how much work you and your designers need to do. It will set the tone for your price point and ascertain how bespoke your design might be. It will also determine who owns the design risk – you or the builder.

You can lose lots of time heading down one path, only to discover further down the track that it's not right for you (often due to budget constraints) and then have to start again from scratch. This can be for a range of reasons, and it's not always the builder's fault if this happens. As clients, we might not realise what we are asking for and the cost impact of those requests. Researching and choosing the right path at the onset of your building project is a crucial step, but we should always be ready to 'pivot' should we need to. Here are some examples of the building paths you can choose.

1. A clean site is a good site, and helping out in whatever way suits you can be really rewarding! When building a home, having everyone on the team working together in sync is the goal.
2. If opting for a custom builder, it's important to take your time selecting the right professional to ensure they have the skillset and capability to bring your vision to life.

Custom or bespoke builders: These are builders who can price your job based on a set of architectural or technical documentation and specifications. In this model you need to engage designers and other building-related professionals yourself.

Turnkey builders: As the name suggests, this type of builder offers a turnkey service, which includes the design and construction of your home. They will have an in-house design team (or collaborate with one) and may have pre-selected options of interior schemes for you to choose from. Alternatively, they may be flexible and work collaboratively with you to come up with an interior scheme.

Volume builders: Large volume builders tend to sell land and home packages with pre-determined costs and designs. These designs are modified slightly to suit your land and engineering requirements, which may incur extra site costs. Often, making design changes will also increase the original price.

Pre-fab or modular builders: These builders operate in a similar way to turnkey builders (they will have predesigned options, but are generally open to customisation within the constraints of their modules). They build your home off site in a factory and assemble it on site over a few days or weeks.

Owner builder/self builder: When you take on the management of building your own home, you need to hire licensed and qualified trades to complete individual tasks. This method allows you to pick and choose what you outsource and what you choose to undertake yourself. Alternatively, you can outsource all work and operate as a project manager.

Lock-up builder: A builder that completes your 'shell', then hands over the project for you to manage the finishing trades and complete the internal fit-out. Some trades, such as electricians and plumbers, need to be on board for the duration of the project in order to sign off on warranties and provide certificates.

②

Top Tip
Be explicit about the completion date from the beginning, and be ready to take advice about whether this is reasonable or not.

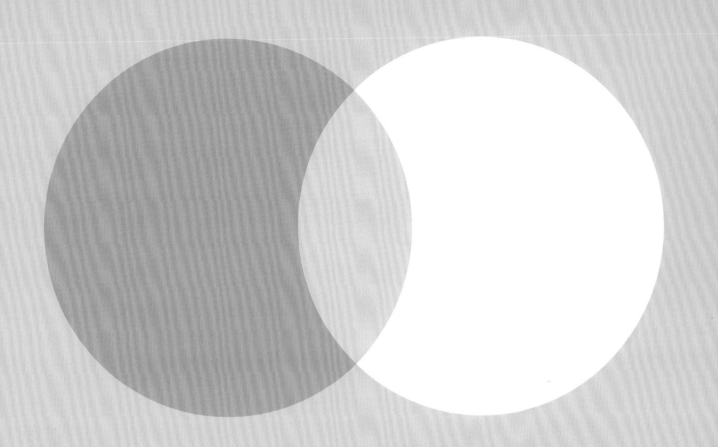

PLANNING
& DESIGN

PLANS & PERMITS

Depending on the extent of your build or renovation, you may need to apply for a planning permit from your local council. Every council has slightly differing triggers, such as land size or planning overlays. These are in place to help local authorities control the level of development happening in a municipality. They also help to ensure that a base standard is met to help manage potential setbacks, neighbourhood privacy and architectural character of the area.

In order to gauge if you need a planning permit, it's important to have a general understanding of what you want to achieve. This can be a challenge in itself, because most of us won't have begun the design process yet, and may be unsure of what our renovation will entail – or if we can afford it! At this early stage it's important to learn about local restrictions and be flexible and open to change.

Firstly, we recommend obtaining your land title and associated paperwork, such as planning and property detail reports, from your local council to see if any planning overlays or sections apply to your property. Secondly, take a stroll around your neighbourhood. Are there homes that look similar to what you want to achieve? Are there double-storey buildings, high fencing, setbacks from the street and neighbours, sub-divided plots etc?

If you discover that you do need a planning permit, then depending on what 'boots' you choose to wear (see page 34), you can either submit a planning application to the council yourself or ask your design team to do this on your behalf. The application should include basic drawings of your proposed build or renovation, with a focus on the look and feel of the exterior and any potential issues, such as overlooking windows.

Top Tip

Ask your design team to fully explain their drawings so you have a good understanding of what they are trying to achieve. Do the plans align with your vision and requirements?

Understanding what plans and permits are needed can require some investigation. This extension did not require planning or council approval as it was within local building regulations, which fast-tracked the process from design to building on site.

To ensure that you're on the right track, you can ask the planning officer at your local council to review your basic design prior to submission and address any problems upfront. For more complex sites or works, you can engage an independent planner to assist you. They will make sure that you have all the required drawings and information for the council to assess your application.

It's important to know that every council operates differently, and they will respond to planning applications within set time periods. When you submit your application you will be assigned a planning officer who may come back to you seeking more information (this is less likely to happen if they have reviewed your design prior to application). They may also determine that your application requires advertising to allow your neighbours an opportunity to comment on your plans. If the response is negative, the council may need more time to evaluate your application or ask you to alter and resubmit your design.

Once planning approval is given, your planning permit drawings will be stamped and planning approval documents issued! These documents may stipulate conditions on your build or renovation, which you and/or your design and build team will need to address.

THE DESIGN

This is a stage that many of us look forward to. It's where we get to make fun, unique decisions about how we're going to live in our home. The design process is complex and brings together a range of considerations, such as regulations, planning permit conditions, architecture, design, creativity and, most of all, functionality.

GETTING YOUR DESIGN RIGHT

Choosing the right design is one of the most important decisions you will make on your building and renovation journey, the results of which you will potentially live with for the next five, 10, 15 or even 20 years – no pressure! Given that design represents so much of the challenge of building, it makes sense that most of us will need someone to come in and help us. But who? There are so many types of designers, and variations in price and service, that it can feel overwhelming when you set out to choose who to work with.

DECIDING WHO TO WORK WITH

A quick search on Google and you'll be presented with myriad options of design professionals in your local area who can assist with your build or renovation. But, ultimately, who you choose to work with will depend on the size and scale of your project and the end goal you are trying to achieve. There's no point paying thousands of dollars for an architect when a draftsperson could have done the job for half the price.

The first step is to understand the roles of different designers and the services they offer. Design is subjective. What you like, others may not, so it's important to find the right fit, both in terms of personality and aesthetics. One of the challenges when working with a designer is that you can never be 100 per cent sure that the finished product will reflect what you signed up for. Do they get it? Do they understand your values and what you're trying to achieve? To some degree, you just need to have faith that the designer will deliver you a concept that you will not only love, but that's also within your budget.

To integrate a modern extension into this heritage house, we hired an architect to marry the different eras, and then worked alongside them to complete the interior design detailing as we built. This allowed us to immediately respond to any issues that arose along the way.

1. The original passageway connects to the extension at the back of the property.

2. The modern extension makes use of the double-height ceiling cavity.

②

DESIGNERS & THEIR ROLES

In residential building there are various levels of designers who have each spent time (some longer than others) in training and learning their craft. Depending on the level of complexity of your project, you might engage any one of these professionals.

ARCHITECTS

An architect is typically used for larger builds and extensions or extensive remodels. They will have spent at least six years in training and then more to get accredited. Architects are design professionals at the top of the ladder in terms of understanding space and building materials. They've put in the hard yards!

Architects will design the layout of a space, taking into consideration the connectivity and flow between rooms. If there is an existing section of the house, they will also understand the importance of this integration. They can manage both the aesthetic and technical aspects of a build or renovation, but this is just a portion of their role. They can also manage the tendering and building process with a builder or contractor, although they are not licensed to undertake the works themselves.

An architect should have a response to the site, your brief and any limiting considerations. They are well practised in dealing with tricky situations and providing creative solutions. They may wish to add their own style and flair or be happily led by you. Make sure you understand your architect's creative process before you engage them. Are they flexible in considering your ideas, or do they have a rigid design opinion?

Generally speaking, this type of design professional will want to be compensated for their time learning their craft, and you can expect to pay between five and 10 per cent of the cost of the building works (or more), depending on who you choose and the extent of their involvement. It's your call to decide how much they are worth to you!

BUILDING DESIGNERS

A building designer is, generally speaking, a more cost-effective option than an architect. The term has come to replace 'draftsperson' to more accurately reflect the role they play in housing developments. Similar to an architect, but with less extensive training, building designers will happily design your home, but for larger-scale developments or more intricate, bespoke designs you might benefit from a more experienced architect.

Depending on where you are located, your building designer may need to be registered, but even if they're not, they will still need to complete their designs in accordance with local regulatory requirements for you to commence your build.

1. For this project, we hired an architect known for their sense of form and drama, which we felt would complement the more traditional house façade.

2. Part of the architect's role is to combine the structural design along with the architectural intent. They are skilled at seamlessly marrying the old with the new.

INTERIOR DESIGNERS

It's a common misconception that interior designers, decorators and stylists provide the same service, but they're actually very different roles. Interior designers are specialists in the way things look and feel. They are qualified to provide advice on both soft and hard finishes and furnishings. As their name suggests, they tend to work on the interiors of a home, providing advice on flow, materials, cabinetry, colour palettes and fixtures and fittings. Interior designers can work in tandem with architects as part of the design team, depending on the size of the project and specialties of those specific professionals. Interior designers can be a great option for re-models within the existing walls of your home. Some are also happy to organise and co-ordinate works on your behalf for an additional cost.

INTERIOR DECORATORS

An interior decorator is an excellent choice if you're renovating within an existing space. They can recommend changes to materials, fixtures and finishes, and offer services including plastering, painting and changing of fittings, such as taps, lights, tiles and baths etc.. Interior decorators are not involved in structural changes to your property.

Top Tip

It is important to understand exactly how much of the project an interior designer will be taking on. Do you need an architect or building designer in order to fulfil the regulatory requirements, or can an interior designer complete this work themselves?

INTERIOR STYLISTS

Interior stylists curate the furnishings in a room. When you see an image in a magazine or coffee-table book, each item will have been procured and styled by an interior stylist, from larger furnishings, such as couches and chairs, to smaller touches, such as the placement of books and trinkets. Basically, they finish and complete the look.

Generally speaking, a homeowner might do this type of work themselves as it's often an enjoyable stage of the process and a chance to really inject your personality! While an interior stylist can perfect a room for a given moment, a homeowner might prefer to allow the space to grow and develop over time.

THE HELPFUL FRIEND WITH A KEEN EYE FOR DESIGN

You know the one, your friend who has a knack for effortlessly bringing things together to look chic and cohesive! Generally, they are not formally trained, but their advice can really help your home shine. Be sure to check in with them on key elements before, during and after the project, but we recommend saving their help for the end of your renovation when you'll be applying the final touches and arranging furniture and other soft furnishings.

An interior designer can enhance a space by selecting the finishes, fixtures colours and materials.

If you don't feel confident furnishing rooms yourself, you can employ an interior designer or stylist to complete your space.

After going to all the effort of building or renovating, selecting the right furniture is the icing on the cake.

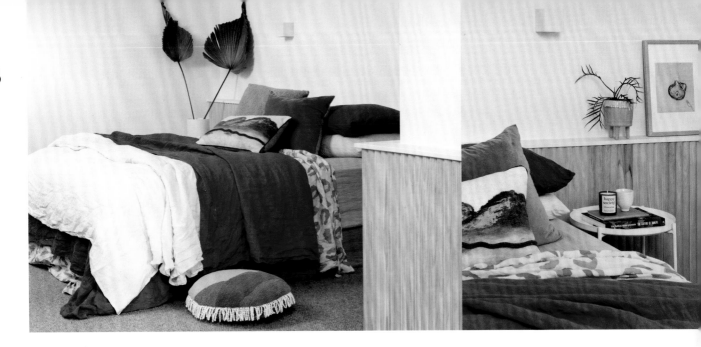

HOW TO HIRE THE RIGHT DESIGNER

Once you have decided what type of designer is suitable for your project, the question becomes which architect or which interior designer should I choose? At this point, we strongly recommend doing some research. Your taste will be individual, and the designer you use needs to interpret your brief and then design a space that reflects how you and the other members of your household want to live. We like to follow the below steps when looking for your new best friend/ designer! Remember, this may be a long relationship that can span years, so a good personality fit is paramount.

WRITE A BRIEF

Expressing exactly what you are asking for is of utmost importance. A good designer will assess your needs as much as you will be assessing them. By writing a clear and concise brief you will demonstrate your vision and the outcomes you want to see in your renovation. You will also show yourself to be an extremely organised client who they want to work with!

INTRODUCE YOURSELF

Every designer has their own process for managing new clients. In the first instance, we recommend giving them a call to introduce yourself and establish their preferred way of working. You want to help facilitate the exchange of ideas and be respectful of their process. This is also a good opportunity for you to assess their communication style and find out if they've worked on similar projects and what their fees might be. You can then discuss the scope of your work and let them know that you'll be sending through a brief from which they can provide a quote.

UNDERSTAND THEIR STYLE AND AESTHETIC

There is no point asking a specialist in Hampton-style homes to design you a minimalist property. While they may be able to technically design this style, if they can't demonstrate this work then it's probably best to choose someone with a more natural passion for the style.

USE IMAGES

In addition to a brief, we recommend sharing three images for each room you will build or renovate, which capture what you're trying to achieve. By limiting the images to three we are being strategic – we want you to have culled to a point where you are really defining the look and feel of a space. Label each image, explaining what you love about it and why. For example, it might be the timber detailing on a wall panelling or a stone kitchen benchtop.

A FACE-TO-FACE MEETING

Prior to signing off on the fee and schedule, you need to meet your designer in person. Can you really work together? Are they respectful of your opinions? Do you get along? It might sound petty, but you'll be working closely to nail down your design, so it's important to know you can communicate with ease!

An interior designer will look at your intent for a space before bringing their ideas together. This bedroom was designed with a young adult in mind, so it required a flexible, yet playful, use of space that allowed them privacy, with enough room to entertain while still living at home.

You might write in your brief that you love your retro couch and want it to be a feature, or that you want to display items you love, such as a guitar or artworks.

THE DESIGN PROCESS

There is a general consensus of how the design process comes together, but each business or design team will approach this in a slightly different way, so make sure their methods will work for you before you hire them. Here's how the process usually works.

THE BRIEF

A document written by you that tells the design team what you are trying to achieve. It should answer the key questions any good designer will have, such as: what outcomes are you looking for? What's your budget? What do you need versus what do you want? How do you want to live in your home? By answering these questions a design team will be able to give you a more accurate quote, allowing you to compare 'apples with apples' when their fees come back. Depending on your chosen delivery model, establishing their fee structure before you sign up is super important.

SCHEMATIC DESIGN

A schematic design is the initial design phase for your building or renovation. If you need a planning permit, your design team will add the necessary details to your concept drawings in order to meet the requirements for your planning permit application. Schematic designs look at big picture items, such as floor space, room flow, orientation, natural light and the look and feel of the exterior. There is no right and wrong on how long this stage can take, and we urge you to take as long as you need to make sure you're comfortable with and excited by your design!

Top Tip

When hiring a design team, it's important to understand how many revisions of drawings are included in their contract, or how many options you will get to consider before making a decision. This is a great time to take a pause, and review your budget.

Originally this house was disconnected from the garden. By reconfiguring the living room, we provided a connection with this unused outdoor area, while keeping within the property's original footprint.

DESIGN DEVELOPMENT

Once you have approved the schematic design, your design team will layer more information onto the drawings. This includes elevations, detailing and information about internal and external finishes. This is also the time to bring on board structural or civil engineers, if necessary, who will provide details on how the columns and beams of the structure and/or large-scale plumbing will function inside the general design. Generally, in residential buildings we don't need to work with hydraulic or electrical engineers because the build is not very complex and the expertise can be found with our plumbers and electricians. This is also a good time to think about inclusions such as smart electrical systems or door controls.

TENDER DRAWINGS

Depending on which building model you choose (see page 35) and if you decide to get your design competitively priced by different builders or contractors, your design team will prepare what's called tender documentation. This is a specialised set of drawings and specifications that enable any builder to price your build or renovation. This then allows you to compare costs because everyone is working from the same set of assumptions and information. If you are managing your own trades, you may or may not want this level of detail. There is cost involved in creating tender documents, but they may save you money in the long run if you work everything out ahead of time. Alternatively, you may prefer to finalise the details with the trades as you build. The more information you supply, the easier it is for a builder to price reliably, meaning you are less open to financial risk.

BUILDING PERMITS

A building permit is a certified approval that your design documentation has been checked and complies with local building regulations. It may require you to provide energy ratings, information on materials, and certificates and computations from a structural engineer. When you require a building permit, you must submit a set of drawn documents and certificates to a building surveyor so they can issue a building permit. Your building surveyor or certifier will issue you a list of what they need and manage the approval.

Depending on which delivery model you undertake, you can determine who is responsible for this process. It can be added to your designer's responsibilities, or in some countries it can be obtained by your builder. Once a building permit is issued, your drawings will be stamped with a unique building permit number, and a hard copy will need to be kept on site at all times. Any changes made during construction should be discussed with your building surveyor and noted on the stamped set on site. Alternatively, the building surveyor may ask for an updated electronic copy to be sent to their office.

CONSTRUCTION DRAWINGS

Your construction drawings form the blueprint that everyone on site must follow. They are simply an updated version of your building permit drawings, with any requested changes by the building surveyor applied. After a final review by your design team, you're ready for construction!

CUNNINGHAM STREET

BUILDHER: CAITY JAGEURS

LOCATION: MELBOURNE, AUSTRALIA

Arguably our most loved BuildHer renovation to date, Cunningham Street holds a special place in the BuildHer heart. Completed in 2017 by Caity Jageurs and her partner (in conjunction with sister Rebeka from BuildHer and brother-in-law, John), the home landed itself on the cover of *enki* magazine (UK) and a range of other publications including *est* magazine (AUS).

With a long family history in the carpet trade, herself 15 years and counting, Caity is no stranger to floorplans and renovations. So when a tired, redbrick residence with undeniably good genes came up for sale off-market, Caity was able to visualise its potential a little more easily than her tennis-coach partner.

Not quite ready, but unwilling to miss out on the opportunity at hand, the couple placed an offer with long terms, which was successfully accepted in August, 2015.

VISION

Once a general's residence during the Second World War, the home's original features were extra special for Caity – she jokes they purchased it solely for its leadlight windows, city view and marble fireplaces. The heritage home had a really great feel to it, even though it was in poor condition. And sometimes the feel is enough for you to know that a home will be amazing to renovate and live in.

Leading the project with her vision, while guided by architects, Caity's goal was to capitalise on the property's northerly aspect and draw in as much light as possible, to create truly beautiful, liveable spaces – something she believes is often harder than it looks.

Caity and Rebeka's vision was to restore the four main rooms of the original home, knocking down the back section and building an extension that would utilise the maximum space of the block. Sourcing inspiration from Pinterest and Instagram, it was all about finding an aesthetic that would suit the property, and then trying to source the right materials.

1. The restoration of original fireplaces provided a beautiful focal point for guest bedrooms.
2. An absolute highlight of this house are the amazing lead-light windows, which, once cleaned, added texture and charm to the bedrooms.
3. The home's extension is all about drama. Tall, raked ceilings and striking black windowframes create excitement as you move through the home.

JOURNEY

Caity chose to tackle the project as an owner builder, which meant she was responsible for the project as a whole and had to liaise with the architect throughout. Caity asked BuildHer Collective to assist with the design process and help nail the look and feel of her new home, which led to many lively family discussions!

Caity had previously renovated another Melbourne property and, comparatively, Cunningham Street was a much larger project, requiring council approval. It took about six months for the council to sign off the plans, which was three months after they settled the property. The build itself was done in an amazing eight months, largely helped by Caity's organisational skills. Rebeka and John were also on site each day to help coordinate the trades. As they had recently built and renovated in the area, they already had a great building team to rely on.

For Caity, sourcing materials for her new home was the most enjoyable aspect of the build, especially the striking, thick marble slab that makes a huge statement in the kitchen. Utilising the BuildHer network of recommended suppliers, along with her own connections working within the flooring industry, Caity's finishes were reinforced by practicality, including a heated slab.

Caity has always loved looking through housing magazines and has a strong sense of design, evident in the pared back and beautiful home she has created. She also talked through her design ideas with Rebeka and mum, Helen, before making any commitments. Helen was very hands on, selecting and planting out the garden and helping Caity choose furnishings, while dad, Mick, was also involved in the build and dropped in at least once a week to make sure things were running smoothly. Caity considers herself incredibly lucky to have such a supportive family.

Caity didn't live in the house for long before deciding to move, but she will take what she learned to her next property. She loved the layout and openness of the home she created, but found she didn't need a two-storey house, and ultimately decided she would be happier in a smaller home closer to her family.

1. Clean lines and a muted colour palette created a calm base for styling. The kitchen sits at the heart of the home, connecting key living spaces.

2. This courtyard doubles up as a light well to carry light into the centre of the home, and add greenery to the aspect.

1. The house was designed to maximise sightlines to the trees, both on the property and the borrowed landscape from the neighbours. The indoor–outdoor relationship was of particular importance to make the house, which was on a narrow plot, feel luxurious in size.

2. The inspiration for the raked roof lines were drawn from the original pitched roof.

3. The increased volume of the living area made a conservative footprint feel more generous.

Perhaps the largest challenge for Caity were the neighbours – on all three sides. The property's rear garaging was accessed via a shared driveway, and the other users were unwilling to look beyond the renovation and see the value the updated home would bring to the area. Caity and her team managed to move past the disgruntled neighbours and continued on with their approved project, but people don't love being built next to and despite attempts to keep everyone happy, unfortunately there were no friendships to be had.

The second major hurdle was the planned site of the swimming pool. Unfortunately, it was rock city below the surface, forcing them to limit the space and size of the pool. They also discovered the remnants of an underground tunnel, which had been built many years earlier. Like most things, Caity took it in her stride, adjusted her plans and got to work.

Finally, the build was on a narrow site, measuring only 6.5 metres (21 ft) wide, while making complete use of the legal height limit of 9 metres (29 ft). This added a technical aspect to the build, as scaffolding was required. Caity also decided upon asphalt shingles for the roof, which are quite common in the US and UK, but not widely used in Australia, so there was an additional process for the team to learn.

Caity found that most issues could be resolved with a little time and patience. Things would pop up, such as the tiler hurting his back, but it was easy enough to find a new one. Her calm and steady approach to building really helped, along with her keen management of the budget to ensure everything stayed on track.

RESULT

Behind the beautifully maintained character façade, you're greeted by an overwhelming sense of space in a wonderfully executed architectural home. Downstairs, there's the master suite, a second bedroom, dedicated study and luxe main bathroom under the high ceilings of the original main roof. Walk past these rooms and you emerge into the sumptuous extension, wrapped in windows. Caity is in love with the hydronic-heated slab, a stroke of genius that allows a minimal look while keeping the occupants more than comfortable through the cooler months. 'There's so much light coming in from the internal courtyard garden, it really feels like the outside comes in. The windows also frame the neighbour's tree: it's just gorgeous.'

Upstairs, there are two further bedrooms and another bathroom, and a living space visible from downstairs via a void, adding further intrigue and treetop views over the roof. Armed with three indoor living spaces, there's no denying the home's family-friendly flexible floorplan.

1. The mid-tone terrazzo tiles in the main bathroom are paired with a marble vanity top, giving this room a sense of luxury.

2. Furniture placement is important to help accentuate the flow of the room. Here, a perfectly sized couch provides lots of seating, while maintaining unobstructed views through the living area.

3. The internal courtyard brought so many benefits to the home including light, additional external space and great airflow through the living room.

TIPS

Caity cites her sister, Rebeka, and the BuildHer community as integral in helping her choose the right materials for her renovation, offering a willing soundboard and a variety of informed opinions at various stages of decision making. This armed Caity with the confidence that her decisions and ideas about features and materials were sound.

Of the process, Caity says it's more challenging and time consuming than you think it will be. 'Nothing works as quickly as you'd hope, there are always hiccups and you're always making new decisions – you have to be flexible.'

The second storey is one of the few misgivings Caity has about the property. 'We created an internal void to provide a wonderful light-filled upstairs area, but perhaps there should have been more of a focus on creating bigger and equal-sized bedrooms. You don't always realise how small spaces are, and you're confined by regulations.'

WHAT'S NEXT

Regardless of external pressures, Caity succeeded in building an amazing family home – which sold well above the reserve price – as well as creating something lasting and noteworthy to inspire and add value to the street.

Caity is about to renovate another Melbourne home that they've been living in – with BuildHer to guide her along the way. It's a smaller, single-storey project on a larger block. Caity is looking forward to creating something a little easier!

1. Wide sliding doors are a fantastic way to encourage indoor–outdoor flow.

2. In-built joinery provides a place to hide all the clutter of daily life. If the vision for your home is one of clean spaces, make sure you plan where everyday items, such as toys and books, will be stored.

THE BIGGER
PICTURE

WHAT'S IMPORTANT TO YOU?

Now, more than ever, is an exciting time to build or renovate a property, as the sheer volume of choices that we see in the marketplace is phenomenal. Construction aside, the options for tiles, flooring, basins, benchtops, vanities and mirrors are genuinely out of this world!

At times, we wish we could build our homes anew every year just to take advantage of all the variety out there. On the other hand, endless choices make it really, really, REALLY hard to pick the right fixtures, fittings and colours for your home because we don't know if we'll still love them in a year or two once something else comes into fashion or starts trending on social media. How do we navigate the best path to ensure that we'll still love what we choose today in the years to come?

It's a lot of pressure!

All too often we hear from women who are trying to renovate over an extended time period. Some of their issues stem from the trouble with trends. Just like the fashion industry, construction styles change and advance over time. And as with all things, some trends are popular while others are not, quickly cycling out of fashion once they lose traction. Sometimes we like to go against the grain and do things we love; sometimes we play it too safe; and sometimes we are swept up in the latest trends only to regret it later. So, where do we begin? We believe that a crucial step to avoid falling into a trend trap is to turn off the noise for a minute and consider our values and feelings.

1–2. The master bedroom and *en suite* are our inner sanctuaries – places where we want to feel special and connected to our surroundings. By selecting the same finishes and colour tones in the walk-in robe and vanity, these rooms feel cohesive and like an extension of the same space, helping to create a sense of calm and tranquility.

3. Here, the two front bedrooms are connected through the use of a similar muted palette and simple styling.

4. Restoring period features, such as ornate fireplaces, provides a link with the past and the story of a house.

YOUR VALUES AND FEELINGS

Renovating and refurbishing our homes is a massive privilege. We may save up for half a lifetime and only get one chance to nail it. There's a lot of pressure to get it right – and naturally so! At BuildHer, we teach the importance of taking things right back to basics and starting with two important and overarching elements that will influence your entire renovation: your values and feelings.

Your values are essentially the building blocks for your design. When we decide to renovate it's easy to instantly start looking at fabrics, colours or finishes (which is completely understandable – this is a super fun part of renovating) and then get trapped in a quagmire of colourways and materials, feeling overwhelmed by current trends and not understanding the best process to follow. By beginning with values, it's easier to consider what you are really trying to achieve.

Looking at our values is also a great way to make sure that our design and the way we use our space actually embodies and enhances the way we want to connect and share moments with our loved ones. Do you love to play sport or games in the garden, or do you prefer to spend your weekends inside on the couch? Is your child an avid reader? Maybe they would love a window seat that makes the most of natural light. Perhaps you like to spend your free time cooking or do you have a hobby that takes up lots of space and needs to be packed away neatly when finished?

Whether you're doing this for yourself, with a partner or your children, assessing your values is a great way to get those around you involved in your build or renovation from the beginning. This isn't just something you alone are doing anymore – it is an opportunity for your family or those closest to you to voice how the new space will be useful to them. It's an important step towards understanding how different values may dictate your decision making and, ultimately, your appreciation of a space.

The way we want to feel in our homes, paired with our value-driven decisions, is also important. Our feelings help inform builders and design professionals about what we are trying to achieve, and if you do employ a design team it will be what they want to know from the start. It is also a great way of communicating ideas if you don't feel comfortable reading architectural drawings.

1. How you want to live and the view lines you want to create are just as important as your feelings. Here, a brick fireplace gives this modern extension a heritage feel.

2. This paved outdoor entertaining space connects to a grassed play area, making the garden both flexible and family friendly.

1–2. Kitchens are the heart of any home, whether you are single or have a young family or older children. Storage, functionality and position of appliances are important decisions when designing this space.

3. Open-plan spaces provide a sense of connected family living, but it's important to consider heating and cooling, extraction fans and noise.

Architecture and design is an emotive science, and your feelings will be different from your friends, family and partner. How you feel in your home will bring forward emotions, and harnessing this skill will lead to a more purposeful renovation and help you trust your decisions when you test them against the following questions:

- Does this design reflect the way I wanted to feel at the beginning of my renovation journey?
- Does this design align with the values I set when I started this process?
- If this design costs more than my budget allows, what can I live without?

For example, when it comes to myself and Rebeka, our feelings and values are very different from each other. I want to feel cosy, warm and safe, whereas Rebeka wants to feel inspired, happy and energised. My values include: a functional space to cook for my family and friends, a living space that has connection with the outdoors and nature, and a sustainable and inviting home where my children can have friends over to play. Rebeka, on the other hand, values a space that promotes connection between family and friends, an outdoor area to lie in the sun reading a book and a semblance of organised chaos that enables and promotes the rhythm of life.

TRY THIS EXERCISE AT HOME

Of course, there are many ways to design a space, but when you understand your values and feelings and how you want them to shape your home, you can ensure the design fits your expectations and budget. The way we like to approach this is to sit down and write out our top 10 values and feelings, and then pick out the top three and rank them. Then ask the other occupants in your house to do the same.

Sounds simple, right? Well, it is, but it might be harder to align your top values and feelings with everyone else's and then rank them in importance. A compromise might be needed.

For example, if your top value is to eat dinner as a family every night but you don't have space for a large dining table, then a translation of this idea might be to create a communal family space that allows each member to pursue individual hobbies and interests in the same room to support family connectivity.

Top Tip

Expressing how you live day-to-day might not come easily to you. Take some time to write down your favourite activities and revisit them a few weeks later and see if they still ring true.

This home has two internal eating zones: a cosy island bench for breakfast and snacks and a dining table capable of hosting large family dinners.

A MASTER PLAN

Many of us renovate in stages as finance becomes available and it's understandable that your ideas change over time as your renovation takes shape. From an architectural and design perspective, however, this can be problematic, as changes to the original scope of your project will have financial implications. To help keep you on track, we recommend creating a master plan at the start of your renovation to capture the overall look and feel you are trying to achieve. Think about each room individually and how they might complement each other rather than compete.

THE PROBLEM WITH TRENDS

We are exposed to all manner of architectural styles and eras that each play a role in determining the design of the home we might now be renovating. Have a look at the variety of architecture around you. It might include older-style period homes, terrace housing, brick or weatherboard homes, bungalows, condominiums, high-rise apartments, low-rise units, duplexes or villas. The list goes on! With so many styles of property available, it's important to consider which trends will fit your property, and which are best reserved for a more fitting blueprint.

If you think you are easily influenced by trends or you err too much on the side of caution, take some time to bring your interior design together or ask for help. These days there are heaps of online tools available to help you visualise the look and feel of your home. Although you might not have the budget to work with particular designers (or any designers!), pulling together an overall aesthetic for yourself will give you confidence and stop you from making rash and rushed decisions, or changing tack halfway through your project.

When you next think about style choices for your renovation, consider their purpose and whether particular trends work for you. You might decide to 'buck' the trend altogether, or maybe you'll inadvertently create the next 'must have'!

Top Tip
Take note of the way you
and those you live with use a
particular space. Observe if the
current space is working well
or if something isn't right.

FIXTURES AND MATERIALS

When we play it too safe, we can find ourselves with a home that skirts around the edge of being sensational and not reflective of our personalities. Other times, we can design a home that is so bespoke to our own needs and style that it ends up reducing future saleability. So how do we find that middle line? How do we choose an aesthetic that we love and that speaks to us as an individual, but also has wider market appeal? We achieve this by making sure that rooms complement each other, by using colours and materials or patterns that have synergy.

Understandably, this can be hard to do if you're renovating in stages over several years. Fashions change and what you liked at the start of a project may now feel dated. For example, you might choose black fixtures in your bathroom renovation, but two years later when you renovate the next bathroom, gold fixtures might be on trend, so the next bathroom has gold taps. As a theme, the two bathrooms in the house don't complement each other. Now add in the kitchen you renovated 10 years ago with brushed nickel taps. You now have three key rooms in your home with different fixtures.

Of course, it is totally fine to have a variety of sanitary fittings in your home, but if the goal is cohesion, then you need to think about the house as a whole and stick to your master plan as much as possible.

A great exercise to do when trying to work out what trends or themes you love is to compile three inspirational images for each room you will renovate. If those images are completely different from each other, a cohesive theme has not been achieved, and you'll need to refine them until you do! Once aligned, these images will help you to explain to a design team and/or builder why you like certain materials, fixtures and finishes.

1. Contrasting dark joinery and light stone were paired in our Bayview house project.

2. Simple details make all the difference: here, an elegant drying rack in the laundry adds a unique touch.

3. A wall-to-wall mirrored shaving cabinet is a great way to give yourself extra storage space, while creating a neat finish.

4. The contrasting shapes and colours in this powder room provide interest to an otherwise practical space.

5. A tiled shelf is a great way to create extra storage in bathrooms.

6. Floor-to-ceiling mirrors help to make small bathrooms feel larger.

DESIGN AND FLOW

When you think about the spaces you want to create or change in your home, it's important to ascertain whether you need to work within your existing walls or if you have the budget to extend and modify wall locations. Whether your renovations are major or minor, your budget and available floor space are going to dictate how extensive those alterations will be. Sometimes it's easy to over-prioritise a 'trendy' spatial design because it's in fashion and we confuse this as a 'need' instead of a 'want'. Think about whether your idea is really the best use of space and value to your home, or if perhaps you've been influenced a little too much by a passing spatial trend.

Here are some examples of trendy spatial design:

BATHROOM WET AREAS

This means the majority of the floor space (including the shower) is considered a total wet area. The bathtub and walk-in shower are adjacent to each other instead of a shower over the bathtub. This trend is becoming more popular, particularly in family homes, because it enables parents to bathe young kids and babies in the bathtub and still have a walk-in shower for adults. The problem is the additional space required to fit a rectangular bathtub and square walk-in shower. Moving or adding walls or plumbing can be a costly exercise, so it's important to weigh up the benefits before committing.

1. Walk-in showers are ideal in larger bathrooms that have good circulation.
2. When space is at a premium, a shower head over the bathtub is a good solution. This bathtub was built using terrazzo tiles with a waterproof substrate.

THE GALLEY KITCHEN

A narrow kitchen where joinery, workbenches and cabinetry run parallel to each other. This is a popular, cost-effective solution for smaller properties where space is at a premium. The downside with this trend is limited storage space and reduced functionality.

THE GARAGE WALK-THROUGH

A corridor that connects the garage to the laundry or butler's pantry. This trend has arisen in newer developments to make it easier for us to carry bags from the car to the kitchen. Although this might sound appealing, you need to weigh up whether this additional space is worth the cost. Is the trade-off worth it? Or would your money be better spent elsewhere?

FINISHES

When you've worked in the construction industry for a few years (as we have), you begin to notice when new trends pop up or even when trends repeat themselves, and this is particularly true when it comes to finishes. For example, in the mid 2000s it was popular to tile bathrooms from floor to ceiling, but this made renovations more expensive due to the quantity of tiles and labour involved. Today, we see more of a balance between tiled and painted walls, and a growing trend of using more expensive tiles in smaller areas to make a large design impact in the space. When thought out properly, this can give your bathroom a high-end finish, while at the same time saving money on extra tiling.

SUSTAINABILITY

Building sustainably is certainly not new, and for many of us it has become a core value when it comes to renovating. Sustainability is now finding its well-deserved place among our policies and building regulations. For example, in Australia, we are now seeing a mandatory 6-star energy rating requirement for new building works and a 'deemed to satisfy' requirement for refurbishments of existing properties, which simply means the building performs more sustainability than it did, within a prescribed set of guidelines.

Obviously a key consideration is your budget. Yes, there are some cost-effective sustainable features you can add to your home, such as water tanks, solar panels and LED light fittings, but they won't afford you passive heating and cooling, nor will they make your house perform better thermally, unless you can afford extensive works, such as the installation of new insulation and changes to glazed windows and doors.

If the sustainability of your home is of utmost importance to you, then here are some easy sustainable features that you can retrofit:

- Solar panel installation to off-set energy consumption
- Solar hot water
- Water tanks to capture rainwater from the roof to flush toilets
- Under-floor insulation (if you have raised timber floors)
- Ceiling insulation (if you have access)
- Double- or triple-glazed windows and glass doors
- External wall insulation (if possible)
- LED light fittings
- Water-saving fixtures and fittings
- Use of recycled building materials, where possible
- Reduction of what goes to landfill.

If you are considering a larger extension, then you have the added potential to orient your space to take advantage of solar heat gain and position windows and doors to maximise passive cooling principles.

Early consideration of sustainability in your home is critical, as it will drive many design decisions. New builds, in particular, carry many sustainable features that can be easily incorporated into the design. In Australia, renovations and refurbishments are more challenging as older buildings tend to lack proper insulation. Conversely, in the UK and Ireland, properties tend to have old wiring, old-fashioned heating systems and thick walls, which are costly to modify.

When it comes to sustainability, your choice of glazing is an important consideration. With a modern extension, the Alpha house performs better thermally towards the rear of the home, where double glazing helps to retain heat lost due to the property's southerly aspect. The original house still needs to be brought up to standard.

MILLER STREET

BUILDHER: MADDIE TIPPENS

LOCATION: MELBOURNE, AUSTRALIA

Hailing from NYC, Maddie and her partner purchased their first piece of Australian real estate in 2014 after securing permanent residency – an adorable two-bedroom single-fronted cottage in Northcote, Melbourne.

Author of *Reading Without Limits*, a book on strategic reading for students, and a school leader supporting youth who have experienced complex trauma, Maddie helps teachers create trauma-aware environments where students can learn to read.

With two children at home, life was just right for the family, but when Maddie fell pregnant unexpectedly – with twins no less – it became clear that the family were months away from rapidly outgrowing their beloved house.

Contemplating building up instead of moving on, Maddie conceded that the best thing for her family (and her own sanity) would be a larger house with an extra-large garden. Working under the guidance of their real estate agent, the family began the daunting process of converting their home into a three bedroom property to maximise their sale price. This required moving the kitchen, while staying within a conservative budget of $65,000, and a five week timeframe!

Thankfully, the renovation was a success and the house was quickly put on the market. Maddie firmly believes the renovation dramatically increased their selling price and afforded them the opportunity to buy a block three times the size around the corner. The positive renovation experience and sale enabled the couple to go big and bold, purchasing Miller Street a couple of days before the final sale of their Northcote cottage. Armed with the knowledge gained from their first successful project, the couple were able to see the potential in their new purchase. 'It was a really gross, run-down house in a great spot, but we had the confidence to see the potential in something that was borderline unliveable.'

VISION

Speaking of their first renovation, Maddie reveals she was a little obsessed with achieving a particular aesthetic for specific buyers while keeping costs down. But there was a defined shift when they considered the vision for their new home. This time around, Maddie wanted the renovation to best suit her growing family's needs. She says, 'I knew we couldn't afford a massive renovation and/or extension, but with the help of BuildHer we were able to narrow down our criteria and pinpoint our vision, which included a cohesive connection with the garden, a highly organised living space so everything had a spot, along with a whimsical look and feel.'

Part A of the build was to gut and renovate the existing floorplan. BuildHer drew up the preliminary plans and Maddie chose all the finishes. Choosing the custom builder who had also renovated their first home, the plan for part B is to (eventually) extend and add an alfresco dining space.

1. Maddie enjoys a moment at her table in the family's open-plan living space.

2. The lush back garden is filled with a variety of plants. The plan is to eventually extend the living space to create a sense of indoor–outdoor living.

3. Maddie included open shelving and drawers in the living area to create storage for toys, books and trinkets.

When Miller Street settled in 2019, the family of six moved into the garden studio for the duration of the build. Soon thereafter, Maddie's one-year-old underwent serious surgery, leading Maddie and her daughter to move into hospital. Despite what could be considered overwhelming life stresses, the family were able to move forward with the build due to Maddie's high level of organisation and forethought. 'The plans were established, the builder was locked in and I had chosen all the stuff you have to choose. I had trust in the builder and my support network, which was the BuildHer Facebook group. I also knew that even if there were surprises along the way, which there certainly were, that we would be able to manage them.'

Maddie admits the biggest challenge with their first renovation were the many unknowns, and her lack of prior knowledge with the building process. 'As a woman who didn't know ANYTHING about building, it was hard to know when to speak up and when not to. Every decision needed to be made almost instantaneously and I had to quickly gain confidence in my own instincts.'

In a refreshing contrast, Miller Street's largest challenge was the endless choice available to them. A lover of interior design in general, Maddie decided on her own palette and rejected myriad other enticing options. Maddie overcame this choice challenge by finding a pattern and sense of cohesion in her 'likes' on her Pinterest and Instagram accounts.

One of their first hurdles at Miller Street was the very low ceiling height. Upon further inspection with the builder, they realised that the covered original ceilings were over one metre (3 ft, 3 in) higher! They were now presented with a dilemma: spend up for high ceilings, or let them be? Opting for the high ceilings (of course), they unfortunately had to lose their air conditioning.

1 & 4. In the main bathroom, Maddie chose complementary tiles and brass tap wear to give texture and depth to the room.

2–3. For the *en suite*, Maddie selected more playful and colourful tiles, but pulled the same tap wear through for continuity.

Maddie's first win was the impressive sale price of their old house, significantly exceeding their expectations after their tightly budgeted, fast turnaround renovation. Proud of the meticulous styling and cleaning work she completed herself, it all paid off. In Maddie's eyes, their biggest win was the purchase of their current home on Miller Street – a real 'pinch me' experience. 'I cannot believe that I was able to buy this house in our current neighbourhood, with no financial help from family. I also can't believe that we lived in a tiny studio for three months with four children and a sausage dog to help make that dream a reality. Thankfully, we had patience, perspective and the resilience to get through it; and I had the confidence in myself to know I could do it.

'I love that our new space is simple. It truly reflects the vision we created: a connection between the interior and garden, organisation and a touch of whimsy. I also love that it was frugal. We achieved heaps on a limited budget, and I love that there's the possibility to do more in the future when we can afford part B. Finally, I love that it is ME. It has art and lots of kids' books. It doesn't look like everyone's house and I like that.'

1. Although still a work in progress, Miller Street's large garden provides a wonderful play area for Maddie's children, including a cubby house and slide.

2. Black steel-framed windows contrast with the warm, internal colour palette.

3. Open shelving and a concealed range hood give the galley-style kitchen a fresh feel, paired with a statement freestanding stove and oven.

TIPS

One of the recurring challenges for Maddie was losing confidence in herself as she made her choices alone. Working in schools, she is passionate about design and architecture, but at times found it another language. In times of insecurity, Maddie reached out to the BuildHer community, leaning on Rebeka and Kribashini's mentorship and the BuildHer Facebook group. Maddie recommends seeking out plenty of feedback on the floorplan before committing to a build. 'I spoke to a friend who knows about construction, so I could check whether or not my concerns were valid. If you pick at every little thing, you won't have a good relationship with your builder.

'I agree with the BuildHer concept that the success criteria for your house should ground every decision you make. Also, research, research, research. With enough meticulous planning, I don't think you need to spend the big bucks to achieve something lovely.' We couldn't agree more.

WHAT'S NEXT?

As Maddie and her partner built the Miller Street house to live in, it's a toss-up whether they sell and start another project or enjoy their glorious final product! For now, they will receive a professional appraisal of their house and then carefully consider their options.

1. With four children, bunkbeds are a must! A built-in bench seat for storage with a cushioned top makes a lovely spot to sit and read.

2. Plantation shutters over the windows frame the views to the front garden and provide privacy from the street.

3. Maddie added playful touches to the babies' room, with toy animal heads mounted to the wall.

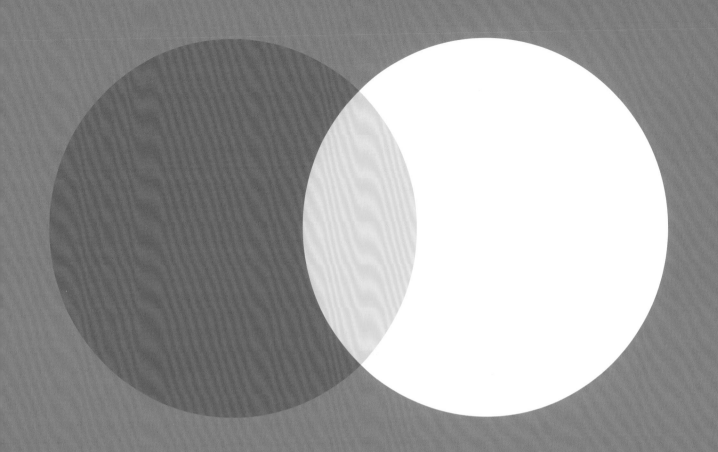

FINDING
INSPIRATION

WHERE TO LOOK

Looking for inspiration for your home can either come easily to you or be excruciatingly hard. Among the BuildHer community, we've met women who feel they've spent their entire life looking for and collecting inspiration for their dream home, mapping out every detail in their head before they even begin. Then there's another group who, no matter how hard they try, are unable to nail down exactly what they want and which direction they'd like to follow.

When it comes to sifting through your inspiration, it's important to narrow down the direction you want to take, but before you get to decoding your vision, take a step back and look at the sources available to you. Once you have a collection of images that inspire you, you can start to filter them to create practical mood boards.

BOOKS

These can be hit and miss, but depending on the type of home you are looking to build or renovate, there are some great resources out there ... such as this one! Naturally, you don't want to cut your book to pieces, so you'll need to photocopy or scan the images you want to use. For bigger-picture inspiration, we like to look at books that explore some of the great architects and interior designers across the eras, along with public buildings that inspire creativity.

MAGAZINES

Print magazines are a fantastic place to look for more tangible and choppable inspiration. They are curated by editors and stylists with a keen eye for upcoming trends, and the content is generally professionally designed and photographed to really showcase builds or products. The limitations here are the long lead times – it can take several years to build a designer's vision and then photograph it, while editors work on a magazine issue months before it is released. As most of us are looking to build classic and not 'fast-fashion' homes, this is not necessarily a problem, but the images can take time to collate if you're looking for multiple styles of inspiration that are not bound to a specific trend.

SOCIAL MEDIA

Instagram has fast become one of the best sources of inspiration for building and renovating. The content is fresh, up to date and abundant, and if you follow the right designers, you'll find posts of what inspires them alongside their own work. You can save images onto digital mood boards and contact people directly with questions about products and processes. We have had great success using Instagram to help people gain the answers to their questions, while also finding inspiration and details for upcoming projects.

Pinterest is also incredibly useful for creating style collections, which you can then link to different products. The only problem is that it can be hard to narrow down your image selections when there is so much beautiful inspiration to look through. Try and pick a minimal amount of styles and stick to them.

Rebeka and I like to source inspiration from different places, both digitally and in print. Once you've collected a variety of images, compare what you like and don't like about them and separate into different piles.

MOOD BOARDS

Once you've gathered your inspiration, we recommend creating at least one mood board. There are no rules when it comes to arranging your images: you might like to put together an overview of what you are trying to achieve, or maybe you'd prefer to create mood boards for individual rooms, focusing on fixtures and fittings, or perhaps you want to concentrate on colours, soft furnishings and fabrics.

We like to start with a mood board for every room to help us determine where we are headed in each living space. As you look through the images you are drawn to, you can become more selective until you are left with a handful of core photographs, which will guide your next steps.

Once your room mood boards are looking pretty schmick, highlight what you particularly like in your favourite images and what you are less keen on in others. This will help you to further refine your aesthetic and draw out what is speaking to your vision. Each image will, generally, evoke an emotion. When this happens, take note of how the image makes you feel and refer back to your values and feelings (see chapter 3). Does the emotion align with how you want to feel in a space and what a home means to you? Do the images reflect what you want to achieve?

When there are so many styles and design choices available to us, narrowing down a concept can be a harder task than initially thought. Once you've refined your mood boards, see if you can find a common theme or view. Perhaps the images are cool and moody, or maybe they are light and bright. Do they have a retro feel, or another thread that stitches them all together?

There are many programs you can use to bring your mood boards together. Powerpoint is easy and commonly used, but Word, Illustrator, Style Sourcebook (a website that collates furniture and material samples), pinboards and sketchbooks are just as good. The method doesn't matter as much as the actual collection and processing of ideas, so use what you feel comfortable with.

Your mood board will help inform your designers about your desired aesthetic. These images communicate design ideas, such as a striking natural stone on an island bench and splash back, a concrete vanity bench, full-height tiles in wet areas and semicircular timber cladding with a stone top.

MATERIALS BOARDS

Once you've created your mood boards, the next step is to take your selected materials and create a materials board. This means selecting specific paint colours, cabinetry materials and colours, splash backs, tiles, flooring, curtains and blinds, and any other fixtures in your home, to see how they all fit together.

A materials board is also a fantastic option for showcasing your inspiration and helping to ensure that what you've gathered is cohesive. We collaborate with many architects and designers, and everyone works differently, from formally presented materials boxes, with samples cut and glued into place with a key on the side, to a box of samples that you can move around and play with.

It doesn't matter how you collate your materials board, the point is to bring your samples together to check that they work, both in terms of colour and theme. Gathering materials may seem like an easy task, but finding cohesion can be harder, as it comes down to selection and composition, which may or may not be a key skill for you.

It is lovely to have a finished collection of materials for a house. Our preference is keep these materials loose in a box so we can play with them. We can switch them out, add details along the way, or replace materials if we need to. We continue to work on it as we build, staying ahead of the trades, but it is our years of experience that enables us to do this, as we understand lead times and potential building issues, so it won't cost us more to continually develop the design. If you are working with a fixed-price build, you will need to select your materials ahead of time and make sure they all work together in the spaces they will eventually occupy.

It is so much fun to play around with materials. We recommend placing all of your samples together, rather than in isolation, so that you can see how they all work together.

Over the page: The James Street house is a hidden oasis in the heart of Melbourne's inner north. Inspired by mid-century architecture, the windows provide an instant connection to the green internal courtyard, creating multiple spaces to interact as a family or with friends.

FUNCTION

THE IMPORTANCE OF FUNCTION

Aside from our values and feelings, functionality is another important consideration when it comes to building and renovating, and most people fall into two camps. There are those who consider the look of their home to be the driving force, whereas others believe functionality reigns supreme. We believe the best approach is to try and strike a balance between the two. We want to achieve our desired aesthetic, but we also need to nail the lifestyle vision for our space.

The role of functionality and our ability to apply it to a space partly depends on the renovation. Do you plan to strip back your entire home and essentially start your flow and functionality from scratch? Or are you renovating within an existing space and executing a lighter refurbishment as needed? A lot of the time our renovations are a mixture of both: key walls might be kept in place, while others are demolished to create larger living spaces. Think about the extent of your renovation and how you can best apply functionality within the spaces available to you and your budget.

The truth is that, for the most part, housing and apartment design reflect a snapshot in time of past lifestyles, society and trends. This means that when you buy an older-style home, which may have multiple rooms, its layout is not going to necessarily fit with how you want to live today. In Australia, for example, it is popular to renovate charming old villas on relatively generous plots of land and build an open-plan extension, particularly in the kitchen and living spaces. In the UK, however, older homes were generally built with small rooms. This was, in part, to preserve heat but also due to increasing urban density as a result of the Industrial Revolution. Today, the flow of these older-style homes no longer suits 21st century living and so we see internal renovations creating open-plan living, to better suit modern functionality.

Functionality in our homes ensures that we make the best use of the space available to us and that no area is 'wasted'. Incorporating a level transition from indoors to outdoors helps to connect these spaces.

EXPRESSING FUNCTIONALITY

When we work with designers, it can be hard to explain what functionality means to us, because it's so individual. What works for you might not work for someone else, and it's the designer's job to understand how you want to live in your home. This means that we need to articulate our vision as clearly as possible to help all invested parties understand our end goal.

When we look at the functionality of our design in a two-dimensional drawing, it can be hard to visualise what we are looking at in 3D. That's okay. Not everyone gets it immediately, and it takes practice to learn how to read an architectural blueprint. If you are working with designers and you think this might be you, communicate this to you team and see if they're happy to mock up a 3D model. These days, many companies use programs, such as SketchUp, to showcase their designs, and we're increasingly seeing kitchen and bathroom specialists using 3D imagery to bring their drawings to life. We believe that through design, drawing, 3D modelling and open discussion, expressing what function means to us is easy to achieve. And while we might be limited by budget, fear of additional structural works or triggering permit processes, these are the things that help us to truly enjoy our homes.

WHAT DOES FUNCTIONALITY MEAN TO YOU?

Our homes should support our functions, not make them harder. Have you ever heard the saying, 'I have a place for everything, and everything has its place?' This is the basis for optimised functionality. Being able to analyse your daily tasks and the order in which they are completed will help you plan your renovation to best suit your ideal lifestyle. To do this, think about how you move around your current space. Walk yourself through your daily rituals and try to pinpoint your movements and how they might influence your renovation.

ENTRANCES

A step that is often missed when thinking about functionality (and therefore a missed opportunity) is observing how we enter our homes. Do you park on the street and walk to your front door? Or do you have a garage and enter via a side or back entrance.

For example:

- When I walk through the front door, I put down my keys and bag, take off my shoes and then walk to the bedroom. It would be helpful to have a tucked-away space near the door or an entrance hall to keep coats, shoes and bags.
- When I get home from walking the dog I am usually muddy, so I enter via the side or back door and would like to have a spot to leave my jacket and dirty shoes.
- My partner is a tradesperson and always enters the house through the garage. They need a place to store work shoes outside, unload tools and leave wet or dirty gear in the laundry before coming into the house.
- I ride my bike to and from work and need a secure lock-up that is easily accessible.

Our entrances set the scene for our homes.
It is the first space our guests see when they visit,
as well as being a common dumping ground for
bags, shoes and keys. Wall hooks are great for
hanging coats and bags, helping to keep hallways
looking simple and neat.

ENTERTAINING

How we like to entertain and connect with others is another important consideration. For example, if you prefer slick, indoor entertaining around a central space, and you want your backyard to simply be a lush backdrop, why build an expensive outdoor decking area? If your climate doesn't allow you to spend longs days and evenings outside, but you like to socialise with friends and family at home, then channel your energy into converting a dedicated internal space for entertaining larger groups.

Kitchens are fast becoming the focus for indoor entertaining spaces, and with the popularity of open-plan living, this means food preparation can become part of the fun. This can translate into a large island bench, which can double up as a breakfast bar or grazing table for platters.

Conversely, we occasionally see overly large entertaining spaces because people overestimate their requirements based on a few occasions a year rather than everyday use. Large spaces are hard and potentially expensive to furnish, leading to budget blowouts.

If a large entertaining space is important to you, but you don't entertain very often, then a multipurpose room layout is a good solution. This might connect a kids' play area with your living and kitchen space, which can be turned over for entertaining when friends come over.

1. With a formal lounge reserved for the original front of the property, this large open-plan extension has three living areas with the dining space connecting the kitchen and family lounge.

2. If you have a large dining table, it's important to have enough circulation space around the table and chairs, to prevent feeling 'hemmed in' while eating.

BATHROOMS

The bathroom is one of the most used rooms in any home, making its functionality super important. Common must-haves might include a hand-held shower rose, hooks or heated towel rails, a walk-in shower or wet space, good ventilation, bathtubs for families with young children and a mix of natural and artificial light for applying make-up.

In recent years, there has been a shift in bathroom design to make them more universal for older generations and those with mobility issues. If you have elderly relatives who visit often or you're renovating your 'forever home', then extra considerations, such as grab rails, wider door frames and a larger walk-in shower might be important to you.

One question that always crops up in our BuildHer community is the value of a guest powder room. Budget aside, this is ultimately a personal choice and depends on whether you mind visitors entering the family bathroom. A smaller guest bathroom is quick and easy to clean and can be useful for older visitors, especially if your main bathroom is located on the second floor.

1. This walk-in shower is a fun addition to the family bathroom, accessible from either end and concealed behind a nib wall.

2. You can easily work storage into your bathroom design through the use of vanities, cabinets and bench seats with space underneath.

GARDEN

Outdoor spaces are becoming an increasing luxury, especially in larger towns and cities where space is at a premium. If you are lucky enough to own a garden, think about how you will make the best use of this space, as well as how often it will be used. If you live in a colder climate, for example, you may only access your garden in the summer months, so perhaps want to avoid having too much greenery, which will become overgrown in winter. A large lawn needs to be mowed regularly, so you will probably want space for a garden shed or easy access to the garage.

If you're a family with small children, you might consider a side gate with access to the garden to stop the kids traipsing mud through the house. Alternatively, if you're a family of water babies and you live somewhere warm, you may go all-out on a pool to save going to the public baths. This may include an outdoor shower and side entrance so that wet feet don't leave marks in the living and dining areas.

STORAGE

One area that is easy to get wrong is storage, and it would be remiss of us not to touch on this subject because you can never have enough! When you think about your storage needs it is really handy to do a massive clean out. Why? Well, for starters it is truly rewarding and will help you feel like you've made a small step towards starting your renovation, but it also helps you make a realistic estimate of your new storage requirements.

The majority of our rooms require storage in one form or another, and this is usually measured in linear metres. Bespoke, custom-made joinery can be cost prohibitive, so be cautious when you are scoping out what you want. Also, try and think of the future. For example, as a young family you might want extra storage in the living room for kids' toys, but as your children grow into teenagers, they might want storage in their rooms or a place to stash sports equipment. Think about items that require long-term storage, along with everyday items that are used multiple times per day.

1. Pool fencing is highly regulated. Locating the pool and deck on one side of the property and installing a glass fence provides a visual connection with the rest of the garden.

2. This recessed wall provided the perfect opportunity for an in-built seat with drawers for storage underneath.

FUNCTIONALITY IN SMALLER LIVING SPACES

If you are living in a small townhouse or apartment, functionality is perhaps even more important because space is at a premium. New apartments are becoming smaller, often with one room combining the kitchen, dining and living space. If you live in an older-style apartment, depending on your body corporate rules, you may not be allowed to move or modify internal boundary walls. Moving plumbing in apartments can be problematic and some councils will not allow you to make changes that affect external façades.

That being said, there are still steps you can take to maximise the functionality and liveability of your space, and establishing your key values will help you work within your constraints. Here are some of our tips:

· Install a kitchen island bench with seating at one end to double as your dining table.

· Build storage into each bedroom for clothing and linen.

· Buy bed frames with legs to provide additional storage space.

· Add tall, thin shelving in the bathroom for towels.

· Make full use of floor-to-ceiling cupboards, by placing occasionally used items at the top.

· Decorate using light colours and mirrors to make your space feel bigger.

· Try and keep corridors and thoroughfares uncluttered.

· Use artwork to create interest and allow you to play with scale.

· Make use of communal spaces where possible, such as cages, laundries and bike storage.

· If you have a balcony or courtyard, try to create an indoor–outdoor flow and feel by incorporating plants both inside and out.

You can conceal joinery by matching the colour with the wall, which can help to make smaller spaces feel more open.

Top Tip

Low-level windows are a great way to catch glimpses of less-expected views.

MAKING
IT ALL FIT

<u>COMPROMISE</u>

Once you begin your renovating journey, you may start to realise that the process is by no means linear! At times this can be frustrating. With so many back and forths, it's easy to feel that with every step forward you take two steps back. Alas, this is part of the story and accepting that there will be hiccups and obstacles along the way will help limit inevitable stress and ultimately lead you to the right place. Sure, there are ways that we can circumvent particular processes, and we can make lots of decisions to speed things along, but, like everything in life, renovating is a compromise – a combination of money for time and money for labour and materials.

This is what makes it so hard. As money comes into play and budgets get blown, emotions can escalate. Referring back to your values and feelings (see chapter 3) will help you through tough decisions. We find that most problems can usually be resolved through compromise and making sure that you haven't bought into the wrong pathways.

Most of us do not have the excess cash to explore different design options, or hire a professional to investigate multiple layouts. In the commercial world this is called an options analysis. The most common options are:

· Extend

· Renovate within the footprint

· Knock down/rebuild.

By this stage, hopefully you know a little more about what you want to achieve. You know how your home needs to function versus how it is currently functioning – and whether that is right for the way you want to live. Now you need to work out whether it can all fit!

Firstly, you need to establish if your vision will fit within your existing footprint, or if you need to adjust the size and position of key spaces by moving or removing internal walls. If your current space doesn't allow for this, another option is to extend. Extensions can vary in complexity and cost, and although they might seem economical compared to a new build, you need available space at ground level; otherwise your only solution is to go up!

Another option worth considering is: 'Should I move house?' Moving home is a big decision. It requires a review of the marketplace and an assessment of whether or not you want to or can afford to stay in your neighbourhood. Often, we hear from women who decide to renovate or refurbish simply because they want to stay within their communities.

In this home, a flexible space near the front door was transformed into a home office. The owner can invite clients over for meetings without them walking through the private family space.

Some questions to ask yourself:

· Do I love living in my community?

· How connected am I to the neighbourhood?

· Can I afford to buy a similar-sized or larger home in another neighbourhood for more/less?

· What impact will moving have on my commute, school zone and support network?

· If I move can I still afford to upgrade my home?

· Can I find an affordable home that meets all of my wants and needs without needing to renovate?

· What are the stamp duties and levies owing if I move?

Ultimately, you will decide whether to stay or go.

When that decision is made, or maybe it's a no-brainer for you, it is time to consider how much space you need. There are standard room-size guides that you can follow in your state/country, but the problem is that they are just 'general ideas'. Your space should be dictated by your needs: how many people will use a room; the tasks that will be performed; accommodation of appliances, furniture and storage; the circulation and flow of the space; and, of course, your budget.

NEEDS VERSUS WANTS

This is a fun exercise to do. Grab a notebook and make a wish list – sounds easy, right? Employ a 'the sky's the limit' attitude and refer back to your values (see chapter 3) and functionality (see chapter 5).

Your renovation wish list will obviously have time and budget implications, so group your entries in a table under the headings 'needs' and 'wants'. This is a great activity to do with a friend, partner or your children if they are old enough.

It's okay to come back and modify the list if you change your mind as you progress, but it is a great reference point, because, in all honesty, very rarely do we have enough money for everything we want.

1 & 3. This upstairs nook is a good spot for a play area, with the feature window providing views to the back garden and trees.

2. A painted steel balustrade was the finishing touch to the upstairs second lounge.

Grouping elements in your wish list into needs and wants will help you later identify in the renovation or building process what you should and should not spend money on. During the planning stage, there are seemingly endless opportunities to consider, but there will be conflicting building outcomes to deal with. Having done this exercise will help you understand what's important to you.

After reviewing your list, take another look and write down your top five non-negotiables. These should be items that if all was said and done and they were not included in your renovation, then you would be disappointed with the outcome. For example: if the kitchen does not have a butler's pantry, I will be disappointed.

We have limited the list to five because it would be easy enough to write a list of 10 or even 20 non-negotiables, but when it comes to renovating it pays to be flexible. Things will pop up and there can be a whole raft of limitations or constraints as to why something will or won't work. We want you to know and understand what is important to you, but also be open to new and creative opportunities.

Top Tip

If you are trying to test the flow and space of your home, take some tracing or baking paper and start drawing bubbles. We use bubble diagrams to help us assess the connectedness between spaces and ensure that the flow will function cohesively.

3

REBEKA'S STORY

Sometimes we need to compromise because we simply can't fit everything we would like into our home. This might be due to space or budget or values. Working on their James Street renovation project, Rebeka and her husband, John, had to reassess their wish list to accommodate more important priorities.

Originally the house was designed to have a basement for the cars and two rooms for their then teenage, almost adult, older boys. At the time of finalising their design their three-year-old, Bear, had an accident and fell several metres on a houseboat, fracturing his skull and collarbone. Thankfully he was okay, but it caused the family to re-evaluate their build, as the large basement would be sitting unsealed for six months in the backyard, and Rebeka and John no longer felt comfortable with that risk.

So, the family of seven made the decision to delete the basement level and the two bedrooms. The priority was ultimately to stay safe and the risk was not justified. There were other factors that fed into their decision: finance – it was far more cost-effective not to build the basement; longevity of the build – a basement would be an ongoing maintenance issue; and sustainability – both Rebeka and John are big believers in maximising space in your home, that is not to create large areas that are used only occasionally, but to try and achieve fuller functionality on a daily basis through flexible spaces.

As a result of this change, and a new baby, several of the children now share bedrooms. As the house is designed with living on one level and sleeping on another, this compromise was the priority. They had the option of rearranging the internal space and having a master suite on the ground floor alongside the living area, foregoing the playroom, but in line with their values, having the playroom to promote connectivity and facilitate family living throughout the day was more important than creating more sleeping quarters.

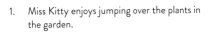

1. Miss Kitty enjoys jumping over the plants in the garden.

2. An in-built couch in the family room means the whole family can hang out together in a comfortable and cosy space.

3. The nursery features a toddler's bed and cot, with a circular glazed window with fluted glass.

KRIBASHINI'S STORY

When Kribashini was planning her renovation after purchasing her first home, she knew the house came with its limitations. It was a good-sized three-bedroom, one-bathroom property, but it was positioned on a half block so the size was always going to be restrictive.

Kribashini and her husband bought it fast and, unlike the million other auctions they went to, they actually hadn't spent much time assessing what they could change as it wasn't on the top of their list. On the day of the auction, the property gods were clearly looking after them and they bought the house at a 'can't walk away from price'. When they moved in, they were pleasantly surprised to discover that the measurements on the real-estate plan had been miscalculated, making the master bedroom and old laundry/sewing room much larger than they had anticipated. Win!

Kribashini ideally wanted a home with a north-facing private backyard connected to the living room. The layout of this house was the opposite: they did have a north-facing living room but it overlooked a large front garden instead.

Flipping the whole house around to try and achieve their ideal orientation was going to be too costly, so they started to look at other ways to make the house liveable for them. When they discovered that they were expecting a baby, their needs and values quickly changed. Their planned timeframe for renovating was immediately cut short, so they made the decision to renovate in stages as they could fund it.

With a baby not far away, the couple's first step was to complete non-structural works to reconfigure the internal spaces to create a three-bedroom, two-bathroom home with a flexible room – think home office/kids' playroom. They also fitted out a new kitchen. During the second stage, they fenced the front of the property to create more privacy. This later enabled them to connect the living room to the front garden to create a sense of indoor–outdoor living. With the addition of two landscaped zones coming off the living room – an outdoor eating space and a grassed area – they were able to make full use of the north-facing aspect. Finally, with the baby's imminent arrival, they bit the bullet and dipped into their savings to renovate the family bathroom, as they knew this room would become a focal point in the house.

Renovating in stages as money became available was challenging and took determination. There were plenty of times Kribashini and her husband felt unmotivated to 'gear up' for another stage of works, or became frustrated because they couldn't proceed due to lack of funds. The house is still a work in progress: the outside walls and trims need to be painted, their master bedroom is incomplete and all new furniture is yet to be bought, but the big things are done.

1. Without the possibility to extend at the front of the property, the living room size was set. Changing the windows to French doors helped to make the space feel larger.

2. This kitchen layout is a traditional triangle format, as the space is too narrow to fit a galley-style kitchen. The idea was to keep it as functional as possible with a full-height tiled wall, a neat 200 mm (7¾ in) stone splash back and 2-pac painted cabinet doors.

THE KEW HOUSE

BUILDHER: ALISON LEWIS

LOCATION: MELBOURNE, AUSTRALIA

Like many of us, Alison Lewis has worn a number of hats throughout her career, collecting experience in a range of complementary roles that have led her to the hard hat she wears now. After harnessing the analytical side of her brain from her early career working in cybersecurity and finance, Alison craved creative stimulation, and so returned to university to study interior design in her late 20s.

While studying, Alison's experiences in residential and display-home property styling helped her pinpoint which aspects of the industry she wanted to work in. Alison eventually quit her full-time cybersecurity role in 2008/9 to pursue her interior design career, while also designing and project managing the renovation of her house in Kew, Melbourne.

TIMING

Having previously renovated a modern industrial-style home in Melbourne's north, Alison discovered she had a passion for residential design and development. So after the sale of their house, Alison and her family spent five months on the hunt for a new space to renovate and call home.

Viewing a 1930's Californian bungalow in the suburb of Kew off-market, Alison took a walk-through video of the home for reference, verbalising ideas for the space as she went along. Afterwards, Alison placed an offer, but it was rejected. As the unsold property moved on-market, Alison and her husband weren't entirely convinced that the home was for them – but they hadn't really let it go either. The home had a beautiful period style and wonderful bones, yet on the day of the auction, they decided they might be rushing into the purchase and decided not to bid, attending the auction for a little closure.

Standing on the busy street, the couple quickly realised how few people were bidding. Seizing the opportunity, they jumped in with a relatively high bid and blew the active bidders out of the water. As bidding ground to a halt, the couple negotiated 45-day terms, and their offer was accepted from their one last-minute bid. What a rollercoaster!

1. With an eye for detail, Alison put together a palette of warm colours for her furniture. Her bespoke coffee table was a must purchase, perfect for the space.

2. With white sheer curtains softening the room, this was the perfect space for a reading nook.

3. Retaining existing features of the cottage was important to Alison, to make the space feel cosy.

4. Unique cabinet handles and soft leather dining chairs are just some of the finishing details that Alison chose for her home.

VISION

Now the proud owners of a Kew masterpiece in the making, Alison had 45 days to rack her brain and create a vision for their new home. She spent most of her time finessing the floorplan, turning dark and pokey rooms into a light, open-plan space.

As an interior designer, Alison is always excited to work with different aesthetics, in this instance redesigning a period-style home with ornate cornices, 3.1 metre (10 ft, 2 in) ceilings and original Baltic pine floors.

Influenced by the desires of affluent Kew residents and wannabe Kew residents, Alison directed the the style and quality of the build towards those who would choose to live there. She quickly crafted an initial concept for the home by taking inspiration from local minimalist interior design companies, referring back to her walk-through video musings and pinning well-executed small homes on Pinterest.

Yet upon moving in, the couple didn't begin straight away, simply ripping up and replacing the carpets and choosing to sit thoughtfully in the property for a while. With only 300 m² (3200 ft²) to work with, and the house taking up most of that space, Alison cites this process as crucial in helping them understand the flow and best use of each space – not to mention the best light.

1. It's all about the journey. Every home you build or renovate will be better than the last. In her daughter's room, Alison painted the walls half height to add colour and a connection to the scale of her little human!

2. In a galley-style kitchen, bench space is hard to come by. Alison decided to use a longer, more narrow island bench to give her the preparation space she needed.

Alison took the building journey entirely at the pace her family could handle and afford, affectionately referring to the stages of the build (to the exasperation of the builder) as stages one, two and three. Little by little, as the couple saved money, they ticked through their stages, taking 2.5 years to complete the renovation.

Alison loved every step of the project from her position as designer and project manager. This was the first time that she had managed and scheduled various tradespeople, but Alison insists that the trusting relationships she developed, particularly with her builder and carpenter, and working through the (many) challenges were her favourite parts of the process, learning a ton along the way.

Feeling supported by her crew, despite the design challenges she threw at them, Alison felt confident to say, 'I appreciate that you've never done this type of detailing before, so how can we try to get the best outcome?'

②

CHALLENGES !

The house itself was an overall challenge. It was affectionately coined 'the house from hell' by the builders, as unfortunately the structural integrity of the 1930's home was compromised by particularly crumbly bricks and termites.

This forced Alison to redesign the renovation as she went along, based on issues that arose through the demolition work. As they went to replace the windows overlooking the north-facing backyard, they found the entire back section had been demolished by termites and was no longer structurally sound. This forced them to redirect funds reserved for a skylight in the kitchen to rebuilding the back end of the house.

Endlessly positive, Alison says, 'That's why we have contingencies!' In a stroke of fate, once they had replaced the back section with new windows and experienced the abundance of natural light it introduced to the space, they realised a skylight would have been overkill.

The other challenge presented by trying to preserve existing features was the havoc wreaked by termites on the pink painted floorboards (as the couple realised when they quite literally fell through the boards at the back of the house). Believe it or not, Baltic pine boards experienced a change in standardised width in 1979, so sourcing their 1978 boards was almost impossible. Unwilling to compromise on attention to detail, it was a definite win for Alison when she tracked down enough 1978 boards to complete their floors, insisting, 'it's the one per cent that makes a difference'.

Witnessing the result, it's hard to argue with Alison's logic. Replicating the subtle art deco façade, internal curves form a large part of connecting the dots from the original house to serene new build.

'I love the finishes – my kit kat tiles! I love being able to pick out small, but cohesive details throughout the house. It's a really calming space for me – the warm textures and materials appeal to me, they make me feel relaxed.'

The curved island bar wrapped in feature tiling draws the eye, while whitewashed boards are illuminated by an abundance of natural light. 'I love that we've been able to open it up. I love the new open-plan floorplan – the kitchen, dining and living space have a complementary relationship.'

Alison is also a massive advocate for practicality, citing her kitchen's floor-to-ceiling cabinetry and the new *en suite* as two of her favourite additions.

1. In this image, a low-height marble upstand is paired with gorgeous finger tiles on the splash back, which are then carried through to the island bench.
2. By transforming joinery doors into the door to her *en suite*, Alison created a seamless continuation of her timber wardrobe across the whole wall.
3. Pulling the finger tiles through to the bathroom and *en suite* helped tie the whole house together.

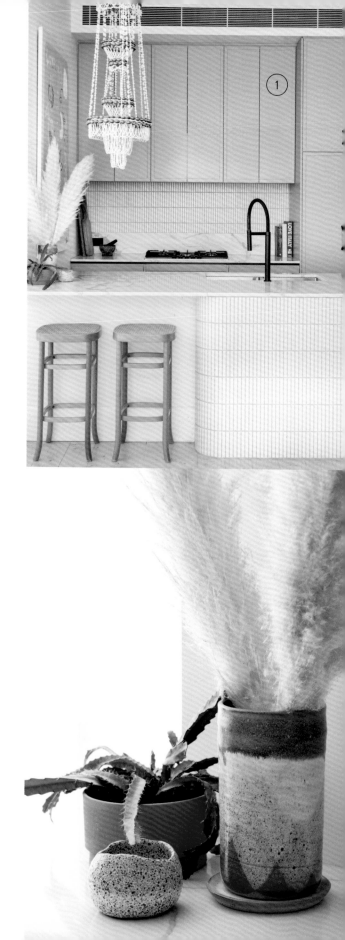

1. Removing old fireplaces in homes can require structural works, which can add considerable cost to your project. If the fireplace is not in the way, consider making it a feature in your home.

2. Most smaller homes don't have space for a dedicated room for hobbies. By transforming a corner of the living room into a reading nook, Alison created a dedicated space for relaxtion.

3. Consistency in colour and style gives this home its luxury feel. Alison continued her joinery into the hallway and added feature timber panelling to the walls.

TIPS

Throughout the renovation, Alison worked hard to ensure that everyone on the build felt involved and that they were working towards the best collective outcome. She never lost patience and was never short with her trades, even bringing her team morning coffee and checking in that they had everything they needed. Alison says, 'My top tip would be to go with the flow. Things are going to come up. I think if you accept that it's not going to be exactly how you envisioned it, but it's still going to be beautiful, it takes a lot of pressure off. Don't get too stressed, there's always a solution.'

A big part of being able to 'go with the flow' is a solid contingency plan and budget. 'I've never come across or worked on a project that hasn't had something come up that meant an additional cost. Make sure your budget and costs are right.'

Alison also insists that a collaborative approach with the builder, designer and architect will help you find the best solution. Last but not least, Alison believes it's important to have fun. 'If you want to renovate, then join in and be a part of it. Have as much fun as you can.'

WHAT'S NEXT

Completing their renovation journey in 2020, Alison and her family had planned to spend three months in Bali, but thanks to Covid-19, their plans have had to change. If there's any silver lining to the pandemic, it's the flexibility granted to Alison's husband's work life as he is now working from home.

They are currently spending five months in Byron Bay on the New South Wales coast. Having just listed the Kew house on Airbnb as a luxury rental, the family are taking the opportunity to experience a lifestyle change while their daughter is young. Renewed lifestyle flexibility is certainly Covid's silver lining. 'We will be scouting homes. If we find something we like it will be a permanent move. Everything has lined up and it's given us this opportunity. The plan is to invest in a property I can renovate myself in the next 12 months, either up north or in Melbourne.'

One of the first guests to rent the home is another BuildHer member, whose own space will be unliveable for 10 weeks, giving her the chance to experience Alison's beautiful completed home.

A small master bedroom can still feel luxurious, especially if the furniture is well proportioned. Alison's decision to use a bedhead with integrated shelving and mixed lighting helps to balance this room, not to mention the adorable existing lead-light window.

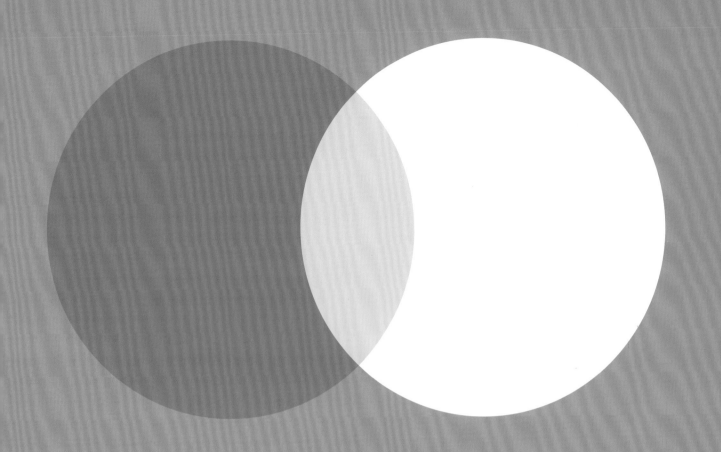

THE ROOMS

A PLACE FOR EVERYTHING

There are key areas in our homes that we need to get right. Each of us have different ways of living and areas of importance. Whether you love to cook or love to sleep, by creating a specific structure and defining principles for each living space, you can ensure that you nail your vision the first time around.

Have you ever been in a friend's kitchen and nothing is where you would put it? Its flow and function doesn't work in a way that is compatible with how you would use the space. The cutlery isn't in the first drawer you open to find it, the plates are up high and you spend your time opening cupboards and looking for things. This is simply because the person who set up the kitchen has a different internal layout and mapping system to you.

The key to getting your spaces right is to have them function in the best way for you and your family and no one else, and this takes thought and planning. Think about what you will do in each space, how it will be used by different individuals and where items should be stored. In this chapter, we will help you map this out.

1. This small bar area is a designated 'adults zone', creating a special place for entertaining.

2. Incorporating built-in bookshelves and joinery allows you to display the things you love. Remember it's okay to not have everything you own on display at the same time. Create little vignettes and change them up every so often to keep your space feeling fresh.

FLOW: INDOORS TO OUTDOORS

The flow between indoors and outdoors is one of the most important connections you can make. This is true whether you live in an apartment, unit or a house, be it a balcony, courtyard or garden. We connect spaces with light and movement, and how we transition through these areas can affect our energy and the way we feel about how our homes function.

Architects often play with the size of rooms. They may compress a space, but then allow the ceiling height to rise, making us feel as though we have entered a larger, more spacious zone. The connection to light and the outside is a big contributor towards these feelings. The orientation of our living spaces and the way the windows connect with the external world can change our moods dramatically. In the Southern Hemisphere, a north-facing aspect provides light all day. This means that in cooler climates you might try to draw that light into your home year round, while in warmer regions you might want to minimise the amount of direct sunlight shining in.

If you live in a family environment, the size of your family and the age of your children can also be determining factors. Generally speaking, a family home will seek to create flow from inside to outside. Not only does this provide a sense of connectedness between living areas, it also enables children to play outside under the watchful eyes of parents who might be undertaking other activities indoors.

(2)

1. Having a garden adjacent to a living space can instantly create an indoor–outdoor zone. Installing full-height sliding or French doors that open onto garden areas improves the connection with the outside, while also allowing you to enjoy the experience of being in a room with a view to the elements.

2. Think about the changing seasons in your garden. In winter, these silver birches lose their leaves, which lets additional light into the living areas. In summer, they are in full leaf, creating shade and lovely dappled light.

Top Tip

Think about the view lines you would like to create. Where will you be sitting or standing and what would you like to be looking at? If you are in an apartment, how will you orientate yourself to take advantage of the best light? If you have a garden view or a view of the horizon, how will you best utilise this?

Top Tip

Think about pathways ... What is outside that will draw you into this space and how will you get there? Is there an eating area or a barbecue that you want to use? Do you imagine using a particular door? Is the pathway from the kitchen to this area convenient?

ENTRANCES

Our front doors and entry areas are often viewed as a focal point of the home. Entrances are the first place you and your guests experience upon arrival, so their functionality and feel is really important. When planning your renovation, think about the impression you'd like your entrance to make on others.

Often, front doors are protected from the weather by a porch or verandah, which additionally offers a line of sight from the street to the front door. Increasingly in modern homes, the trend is to have an anti-front door (where the entrance isn't protected), but we personally think we need a place of cover as we enter to protect us from the elements and allow us to put down bags while we fossick around for keys.

Once inside, the hallway is most often the place to dump the remnants of your day from the outside world. Think about what will facilitate this transition from the outside to indoors. You might like to add a hallway table for keys, hooks for bags and coats or a shoe rack to sit under the table. If space allows, a walk-in cupboard is a great solution for hiding away outdoor gear that might otherwise clutter your entrance and detract from the flow of the front door through to your living areas. Also, see mudrooms on page 187.

1. This entrance is located to the side of the house and is reserved for family and friends. Having separate entrances creates a sense of belonging to an inner circle and allows you to allocate specific storage to the people who use it.

2. This image shows the traditional front entrance to the home and the 'family and friends' entrance just off to the side. The step down denotes a difference between the old and the new, adding a sense of drama and signifying a change of zone.

3. Older-style homes are often dark. Skylights, such as the one featured here, allow you to pay homage to the heritage of a property, while modernising it to be lighter and brighter.

Top Tip

It's lovely to have a dedicated zone to welcome visitors into your home, but if space is critical and people are entering straight into the living

room, consider a privacy partition to demarcate the entry. This might be a decorative screen or a low bookshelf with indoor plants.

LIVING ROOMS

Our living zones can be open plan or a separately partitioned room based on the period, style and size of your home. Alongside the kitchen, it is one of the most important spaces to consider when renovating as it is used by everyone. This is where informal living takes place: watching TV, entertaining and relaxing. It is a space that requires real flexibility to accommodate a range of activities and tasks. In terms of zones, we might think of our kitchen, living and dining areas as three spaces that require fluid connectivity.

A key to successfully designing your living space is to assess early on what furniture you intend to include and where it will be placed. Will you be using pre-existing furniture or buying everything anew once your renovation is complete? Think about the size of your couch, how many additional chairs you need to host guests, where the TV unit and any bookcases will go, and allow for ample circulation around furniture that might be placed in the middle of the room.

If you have the space and budget, a second living room can make an amazing extra breakout space, working particularly well for larger families with children of varying ages. Depending on what stage in life you are planning your renovation, think about how your house will work for you now and into the future. Those little kids will grow before your eyes, and their needs will change! We know some teenagers want their own sanctuaries away from the family, which is understandable. Young adults often want to forge their independence, so an extra side entrance into this second living area allows them to enter the home without interrupting the entire household – for everyone's benefit!

Centering rooms around in-built features, such as fireplaces and joinery, is a nice way to ground the room. This living space in the Bayview house was reserved for more formal occasions, with doors connecting the space to the larger, informal living area.

Top Tip

Think about the way you use your living room now and how it could be improved. What are the moments you want to create? How will you move around and through the space to complete your daily activities?

①

②

1. Custom-built floor-to-ceiling joinery provides lots of storage in the playroom at James Street.

2. A second lounge was important to give everyone their own space. Multiple activities can happen concurrently in different areas of the house.

3. The large, custom-built, u-shaped couch in the playroom allows lots of bodies to be in the room at the same time. When the kids are playing, the room can be covered in toys, but come bedtime the clutter can be quickly packed away, instantly turning the room into an adults' retreat.

DINING ROOMS

The dining room is directly correlated with that particular function, although nowadays, more often than not, we find that homes are built with an open-plan kitchen, dining and lounge all rolled into one. If you do have a dedicated dining room, chances are you rarely use it. Perhaps your plan is to knock through the dining room wall to connect it with the kitchen and/or living room? Or perhaps the space is better transformed into a bedroom or study and the dining table moved into the main living space if there's room?

Regardless of where your dining space is located, its size and function should correlate with the dimensions of the dining table you plan to use and how many seats are required. Is your dining table round, rectangle or square? Will there be enough circulation space once additional furniture, such as a sideboard, buffet or cabinetry, is in place? Remember to think about both day-to-day living and those seasonal celebratory events, such as family dinners, birthday celebrations and Christmas.

Finally, consider the adaptability of the space and if a trade-off is required. Again, this falls down to understanding your values, how your family functions and whether you can build or renovate a home which facilitates the way you would like to live.

There are so many ways dining tables and eating areas can be created. If you don't have space for an actual dining table, then perhaps you could add a built-in bench seat? Alternatively, a kitchen workbench could double up as a breakfast bar with stools underneath. Perhaps you don't have space for both an island bench and a table, so the dining table could be designed as additional bench space?

1. A breakfast bar positioned at the end of a kitchen island bench is a great way to enjoy informal meals and snacks.

2. Hanging a large pendant light over your dining table can add volume and grandeur to that space. Round tables encourage cross-table talking but do require a more square-shaped dining area.

If you live in an apartment or unit and space is at a premium, then consider a fold-out table that can be housed against a wall. Kribashini spent a few years living in Japan, where this is a common feature due to the minimal size of apartments.

Again, joinery can be a large part of this equation. If you have a small kitchen, a buffet cabinet is a great solution for housing tableware and glassware. Buffet cabinets can also help demarcate an area, helping to visually separate the kitchen and dining room in an open-plan space. Incorporating different-height furniture helps to layer a space, allowing you to create visual interest through styling.

Of course, in an ideal world we would have different eating areas depending on the occasion: breakfast at the kitchen bench, family dinners at the dining table, informal entertaining in the garden, a cocktail and cheese board next to the bar and a sneaky after-dinner snack with a cuppa on the couch. There are so many, many ways to eat in one home!

1–3. The James Street house has three eating zones: an outside dining and entertaining area, informal breakfast bar and formal dining room table. Having the luxury of a variety of spaces available means that family members can undertake different activities at the same time. Each zone is connected but flexible.

4. Kribashini's dining table helps to separate the kitchen from the living room, while still making the overall space feel cohesive.

THE KITCHEN

No matter how many women we speak to, most of us agree that the kitchen is the heart and soul of the home, and arguably the most important room in the house. This is the room where you will cook for family and friends, and, if designed well, it may also be the space where you entertain guests, work from home or help the kids with their homework.

When designing and building a kitchen, you need to think about the overall flow, aesthetic and the sequencing of the build. Most of us have myriad ideas about the way we want our kitchen to look; however, functionality is really the key. If you get this wrong, certain elements or features will start to annoy you and ultimately reduce your enjoyment of the space.

Kribashini and I often joke about how different our kitchens are, namely because we are not the same people. Yes, there are some overarching principles, but an individual's kitchen and how they use it is quite personal. This is governed by many factors, such as the amount of meals you cook (do you need a large pantry to accommodate tins, dried goods, spices and condiments?), the type of cooking you do (does your microwave get a better workout than your stove?) and the other tasks you may undertake in that space.

The most important aspect to consider when building or renovating a kitchen is that you've allocated enough space in your floorplan. This might mean working with a kitchen designer to help you map out your design. We urge you to do this at a stage when your floorplan is still flexible, so that you aren't locked into a particular location for cupboards and appliances, giving you the opportunity to make the most informed decisions.

By examining the key areas in your kitchen, as well as thinking about how you would like it to look, feel and function, you will understand how your kitchen will operate before it is built. When combined gracefully, each of these key elements will ensure that your kitchen is a winner.

A light, calm and neutral palette was the aim for this kitchen. Overhead cupboards and a butler's pantry allowed for lots of storage, while the long island bench is perfect for cooking and entertaining.

KITCHEN LAYOUTS

There are several shapes that a kitchen can take, such as U-shaped, L-shaped, galley or island, and what you choose will be partly driven by the space available. There are advantages and disadvantages to each style, so it's important to ascertain how and if a particular shape will work for you.

The working triangle between the stove, fridge and sink is really important. Ideally you will have no more than a few steps between each one. The way you move among these appliances will determine your kitchen's usability. We like to think of cooking as a kind of dance – when the flow and rhythm work well, then it's graceful and elegant, but if the path is blocked by an item, or the space between appliances is too large, then it can reduce functionality. This experience, good or bad, is intensified when there are several people cooking in the kitchen at the same time.

1. A walnut veneer was used to add natural texture and depth to this home which otherwise has hard surfaces of stone, terrazzo and steel. The layout incorporates a butler's pantry hidden from the main area.

2. The spatial relationship between the kitchen and dining area should be considered. Both areas need to work harmoniously to encourage flow.

3. A bar area was included in this u-shaped kitchen. Deep cabinetry tones and a mirrored splash back intensified the moodiness of this area.

THE BUTLER'S PANTRY

If you have room for a butler's pantry and you're a lover of clear spaces, then we can't recommend them enough! It's the perfect place to hide away benchtop appliances, utensils and all the unsightly things. Controversially, we love a butler's pantry with a dishwasher, so used pots and dishes can be stacked and dealt with later.

Butler's pantries range from walk-in food pantries, to larger spaces that look more like a second kitchen! We think a happy medium is best, but, of course, it all comes down to space and budget, as well as the functionality of the space. Will more than one person be using it at a time? If you are at the sink or the dishwasher door is open, can you access the rest of the space or are you preventing anyone else from using it? If you are cooking, will it be practical for you to walk in and out of the area? Once you have nailed these aspects, you can start to think about all the other kitchen clutter you can hide away.

1. Open shelves allow for easy storage, but they need to be kept clean or they will clutter a space.

2. Think about your storage requirements and the packing and unpacking of the dishwasher. Sinks need to sit next to dishwashers both for plumbing purposes, but also for the natural rhythm of the workspace.

3. Rebeka is a massive fan of the butler's pantry! All those children eating and using dishes makes it a saving grace. Her pantry is a place to hide the daily clutter that hasn't been put away, as well as accommodating a dishwasher and large sink. On a practical level, the kids know to stack their used dishes in this area, which is hidden from the main kitchen. Kid-friendly food, such as breakfast cereals and snacks, are placed on low shelves so the kids can help themselves.

4. If you don't have the space for a butler's pantry, then a well-apportioned pantry cupboard with pull-out shelves might be a good solution. Internal shelving allows you to hide away unsightly appliances such as kettles and food processors.

KITCHEN APPLIANCES

Before you start chasing your way down a rabbit hole of branded appliances, the first thing to think about is the size and type of appliances you want to install and how they will fit into your layout. People tend to have very definite ideas on what appliances they use. In general, a kitchen will contain a fridge-freezer, stovetop, oven, rangehood, microwave and dishwasher.

You can choose to have these built-in or not. Building the appliances into the joinery will give a more streamlined finish as they will look like pieces of cabinetry, but this does come at a cost. It is more expensive (in both time and the materials needed to build them in) and limiting (in terms of the available products) to use built-in appliances. Think about where they will be placed, and if their visibility is important to you.

OVENS AND STOVETOPS

Some of your more important decisions will involve the oven and stovetop. Do you want a tower oven or will it sit under a workbench? Can you cook with just one oven or do you need two? Do you prefer a standalone appliance or for it to be in-built? What features does it need? Or is it actually an AGA you really want?! So many decisions! Try to think about what you cook with now, what you would like to cook with and what is convenient and inconvenient.

Stovetops can be gas or electric or both. Gas cooktops are often preferred by those who like to use a wok and have better control of heat, but they can be harder to clean and require a gas connection. Induction runs off electricity and requires special pots and pans. They are generally easier to clean and cool(ish) to touch after they have been used, making them more family friendly.

KITCHEN JOINERY

Our choice of joinery can add massive cost to a project. The style, quality, quantity and fine details can make a huge difference to the overall price of a build, but it can also affect how you feel in a space. Again, the most important thing to consider is functionality. If it's pretty but it doesn't work, you have a very costly fail on your hands.

Start by asking yourself questions. How will you use cupboards, shelves and drawers? What will you keep in there? Pots, pans, tupperware, bins, cooking utensils? Are drawers your jam as you like to throw everything in and forget about them? Do you have a pile of benchtop appliances that you would prefer to hide away? Or do you like open shelving to display cookbooks and colour-themed appliances? Once you have ascertained what best suits you, your plan will start to take shape.

The method in which your kitchen is manufactured and installed is the final cost implication, and for this consideration you really need to think about how handy you are yourself. A custom-designed, fully installed kitchen will be the most expensive, while an off-the-shelf DIY flatpack will require less of your hard-earned pennies. Where you sit in the spectrum of DIY is totally up to you – the principle of building is the same as most things: the more you pay other people to do the work, the costlier that process will be. In addition, if you select more expensive materials, the higher you will drive your costs. For a forever kitchen this could be perfectly acceptable, but understanding your priorities and budgets before you start to plan will help to alleviate the frustration of unrealistic expectations!

Alternatively, you can spend more on cabinetry or joinery and, if you are confident, install it yourself. Many suppliers are happy to hand over all the required elements, then leave you to put it all together. Over the page, we look at what you need to consider before venturing down this path.

Top Tip

There is a hierarchy of costs in joinery, and understanding this will help you to design within your budget. For example, cupboards are cheaper than drawers because of the mechanism costs, while laminates are the most cost effective, followed by vinyl wrap, 2pac and then veneer. There are obviously many, many variations in between.

1. You can add texture to joinery by staining timber a solid colour.

2. In this kitchen, white-washed timber creates a soft feminine look. It is paired with brass tap wear.

3. Here, the joinery handles are in the same finish as the cabinetry doors. Their shape is a nod to the era that inspired the joinery.

4. There are many finishes and textures you can incorporate into your joinery. A wire mesh on these doors creates a 'breathable cupboard'.

5. Custom timber veneer battens add texture and warmth to an island bench.

· Suppliers usually make joinery to a standard size, so do your research ahead of time to find out if their measurements will fit your kitchen design.

· If you are replacing a kitchen, think about the location of the existing plumbing points. Keeping appliances in the same or a similar location will often save money, but if their position doesn't suit your needs, then perhaps it is worth investing in moving these services.

· Source quotes from electricians and plumbers before you begin. These are licensed trades and need to be completed by someone who is registered to do the work. This is a great opportunity to talk through the required job, either on a plan if you are building a new space or in the space if you are renovating. Nut out any issues that you might come across ahead of time.

· Make sure you start with a level surface before you build your carcass. Adjustable legs will also help keep cabinetry level.

· Creating the boxes should be the 'easy' bit. Always follow the instructions and perhaps lighten the flat-pack 'mood' by playing upbeat music while you work. You could even crack open a bottle of wine!

· If you are not confident with DIY, perhaps employ a carpenter or joiner to help with trickier elements, such as fillers (which go between the wall and the cabinets) and benchtops. Both of these areas often need scribing (cutting in) as the walls will be out of line or not plumb.

CUPBOARDS AND DRAWERS

The majority of off-the-shelf cupboards and drawers come in standard widths, but if you are using a custom joiner you can obviously make them any size you like. Think about their location and how you will use them in your new kitchen. Your sink will generally have a cupboard underneath, and if you have a dishwasher this should be located next to the sink. The location of the cutlery drawer and pantry is important as they are in high use, and you might like to have deep drawers for pots and pans located near the oven or stove.

FINISHES

There are several types of joinery finishes used in the kitchen.

· Laminate: a durable, cost-effective finish that comes in a range of colours.
· Vinyl wrap: also durable and cost effective, vinyl wrap is good for using on a profiled door, as the vinyl will form to the correlating shape.
· 2Pac: a two-process paint finish that can be opaque or applied clear over a timber or timber veneer product. It gives a hardy finish, but can be prone to chipping.
· Solid timber: a costlier finish that still needs to be painted prior to use. You can achieve many profiles and custom finishes with solid timber.
· Black marine plywood: a hardy and cost-effective solution, but with limited colours and finishes.
· Timber veneers: a thin slice of timber laminated onto a substrate to achieve a timber aesthetic. Timber veneers still need to be finished with either paint or 2pac.

When choosing your finishes, it's also important to consider what will work for you on a day-to-day level. For example, if fingerprints bother you then stay away from matt black or overly dark joinery, as they are known to show up all the marks.

HANDLE LOVE

Handles are a great way to add interest to your joinery without adding massive expense. They come in many materials, such as timber, metal, ceramic and leather, and you can easily make them a feature or keep them refined or hidden. With so many options, it's easy to wander down a rabbit hole!

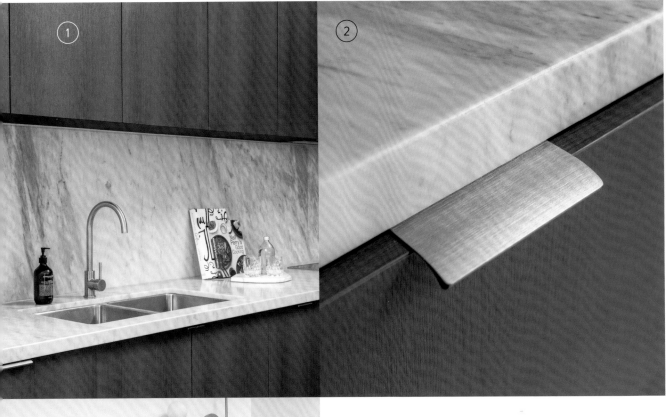

1. Here we see a pop of brass carried through the joinery handles to the tap wear. This adds a lovely accent colour and warms a cool, grey space.
2. The handles are concealed finger-pulls, which work beautifully with the design.
3. Marrying the lighting, styling and handles allows for a cohesive and harmonious look.

BENCHTOPS

A key element in any kitchen – of which there are many styles to choose from – your choice of benchtop will inevitably make a big impact. Here are some of the materials you can choose from.

· Laminate: one of the easiest and most cost-effective materials to work with, but prone to scratching and less durable than other materials. There are many colours and finishes to choose from.

· Reconstituted or engineered stone: made from resin mixed with aggregates, this is generally a durable material in terms of marking and longevity. As it's manufactured, the colour and finish should be consistent. You can choose between a solid tone or flecked colours.

· Porcelain: a relatively new kitchen product, porcelain tiles are printed and sealed. It is a hardwearing material, but check the installation costs as they can be more expensive than traditional stone.

· Natural stone and marble: beautiful materials available in natural colourways, but can be hard to maintain depending on the particular stone or marble you select. Consider using a sealant to improve the look and lifespan as citrus and oils can easily stain.

· Solid timber: provides a lovely finish, but timber and water are not natural friends, so make sure you learn how to care for your benchtop. Timbers need to be treated with food-safe oil or polyurethane (ideally every year) to maintain their look, so make sure you consider the ongoing maintenance before heading down this path.

· Tiles: once fashionable in the 70s, tiles have made a comeback! Be mindful of grout lines, as they stain readily and can be hard to clean.

· Granite: the stronger, more durable friend of reconstituted and natural stones. Granite is incredibly hard-wearing, but has a more limited colour palette.

· Stainless steel: this material has made its way from commercial kitchens into our homes. This is obviously the chef's favourite and can be installed to seamlessly continue into the splash back.

SPLASH BACKS

The splash back (or back splash) is the section of wall behind the stovetop. Importantly, it needs to be both fire retardant and water resistant. Generally speaking, you can use the same material as your benchtop and add a glass panel over the top. This can vary from clear or painted glass to mirrors. Think about what will best suit the style and tones of your kitchen.

A kitchen does not have to be too serious, but you will live with it for a long period of time, so our general rule is to follow what you love and not the trend of the moment.

The Bayview kitchen was designed for family and entertaining. The stone benchtop was always going to be the hero of this space.

If selecting stone, make sure you always view it prior to purchasing as it will vary a lot from the samples. We originally selected a different stone for this benchtop, but when we inspected the slab it didn't meet our expections, so we kept looking until we were happy.

Top Tip

You will view your kitchen front on most often, so print the elevations before you start and colour them in with pencils, watercolours or textas. This will help you see how different colourways will work together.

Installing light-coloured cupboards above benchtops can help to make the space feel larger, but you can also experiment with open shelves, ledges and tonal cupboards.

BATHROOMS

Bathrooms can be one of the most fun but also one of the most challenging rooms to build or renovate, due to the staging and co-ordinating of various trades, fitments and plumbing requirements. It all starts with a clear vision, brief and design, which will direct the project and team. When designing your dream bathroom, you need to understand the requirements of those using the space. One of the key elements to think about here is access for people who might have mobility issues later on in life.

Essentially, all bathrooms are about combining the following items: the vanity sink and mirror, shower, bath and toilet. Yet there are so many scenarios of how this can be achieved, it can seem like an epic task! If you are renovating, then begin by identifying where the plumbing is currently and what it is about the layout you would like to change. Moving plumbing isn't necessarily hard if you have a lot of underfloor clearance; however, if you are on a slab or in an apartment, then it may be prohibitive. If this is you, then try sketching up what you would like to achieve, and then have a fallback plan which keeps all the plumbing positions in the same location.

The trades required to install or renovate a bathroom can include carpenters, plasterers, painters, joiners, electricians, plumbers, tilers, caulkers and glaziers. Many of these trades need to come back several times throughout the process. For example, the plumber will need to rough in (put the pipes in the wall) before the plastering and then return at the end of the process to fit the fixtures. Organising the co-ordination of these trades, and having the correct materials on site when required, is critical to keeping costs down. It can be expensive and frustrating to get people back many times to do a job that is not ready, so make sure you understand the process before you start, to facilitate a speedy renovation or build!

You might have heard that bathrooms are one of the most expensive areas of the house and this is purely because you need multiple water-resistant materials and qualified trades to install them. Each trade will complete small sections of the renovation over a series of days, and every return trip adds to the overall cost, especially if your schedule is delayed by trades letting you down or materials arriving late. If you are hiring individual trades yourself, make sure you lock them in ahead of time. Conversely, if you are using a builder make sure you understand their timeframes ahead of proceeding with the job.

1. This family bathroom includes space to sit near the bathtub and ledges for styling, both of which were included in the concept design.

2. The rounded mirror above the sink adds an element of fun to this space.

3. Wall hooks are great for towels and robes. These hand-made ceramic hooks add interest to a white wall.

4. A powder room can be a lovely, elegant space. The basin in this image is freestanding and does not require joinery. The tones are neutral to create a calm space.

5. The pink sink adds a little fun to this space. An arch-shaped mirror sits on top of the tiles and carries through the playful tone.

6. This family bathroom allows for ample storage in the vanity drawers. Maximising the space and the roofline allowed northern light to filter in, along with the opportunity to install tall mirrors with feature lights.

A sample bathroom build might follow the following process:

· Demolition or stripping out the space
· Repairing any structural work or water damage to the timber – this can also include dropping the floor joists to allow for level tiles, or raised floors for in-built showers
· Plumber rough-in – installation of pipes and services
· Electrical rough-in – installation of wires to power points and lights (we like the electrician to work after the plumber as it is easier for them to run wires around pipes instead of the other way around)
· Floor fit-out
· Plastering and sanding of the walls and ceiling
· Painting of walls and ceilings (we like to do this before tiling, but it can also be done afterwards)
· Waterproofing
· Plumbing of built-in bath, if you're having one. A free-standing bath will be installed after tiling
· Tiling and grouting
· Installation of vanity and cabinets
· Depending on whether there's an underslung sink or not, vanity tops can usually be measured now.
· Final fitting of electrics and plumbing including lights, powerpoints, taps, bath and sinks
· Installation of shower screen and mirrors
· Final cleaning and styling.

Although the James Street family bathroom is rather narrow, the layout afforded a built-in bath at one end and shower at the other. Large drawers and a mirrored cabinet allow for lots of family storage and a clutter-free space. Horizontal hand-glazed stacked tiles add variation and warmth, along with the terrazzo flooring, which runs up and over the bathtub. Keeping the theme tonal and consistent creates a calm environment.

Top Tip

A walk-in shower with a hose is a brilliant addition as it has so many uses: washing children and pets, watering plants, cleaning the shower and keeping your hair dry. Consider this type of fixture for maximum flexibility.

Top Tip

Place plug sockets in one of your drawers for easy access to a hairdryer and straightener without the trouble. If you use an electric toothbrush think about power in your mirrored vanity, too.

The built-in versus the freestanding bath is a popular debate. People seem to be very solidly in one camp or the other. The pros for a freestanding bath are that they look lovely, they can be easier and more cost effective to install and take less time to complete. The built-in bath creates a different aesthetic, requiring more co-ordination with the trades, but it is arguably easier to clean as you don't get water between the bath and the wall and it has a ledge around it, which you can use for styling. We actually like both and will often recommend either based on the available space in a bathroom or who will be using it most. That is the magic of building – there are so many wonderful options to explore. It's up to you and your values!

Top Tip

If you plan to include a skylight in your bathroom, think about its location early on in the renovation process. We like to place them over the shower where possible, but it's more important to have a natural relationship with the room as a whole, providing light where needed.

1. This free-standing bathtub is a feature in its own right. The rounded corners juxtapose the square tiling on the floor and walls.
2. This bathroom incorporates a built-in bathtub with an overhead shower – a great solution for bathrooms with tight floor space.

THE MASTER BEDROOM

The master suite is one of the key spaces in a house that provides a retreat from the world. The place where we sleep and rejuvenate can be as simple as a room with a bed and bedside tables, or it can be more extravagant with dressing areas, walk-in wardrobes and an *en suite* bathroom.

The size of your property and scale of renovation will dictate the size of your master bedroom, but at BuildHer we see many designs that come complete with walk-in robe and *en suite*. These are spaces that we commonly build, and we can afford to be a little more creative as they are private and personal.

Obviously, the master should have room for a bed, bedside tables and potentially a chair, with either built-in robes to house your clothing or the lovely walk-in. We think a full-sized mirror is also a must. The *en suite* or private connected bathroom is of major appeal when selling a space.

The master bedroom is all about creating a sanctuary. The primary function of this room is a place of rest, but it may also be a space where you read, watch TV or study, so think about where and how you will enjoy these activities.

1. We like to create a retreat that has its own style and flair with a cohesive palette. Here, the addition of a headboard creates opportunity for styling and greenery in a moderately sized room. The strapping on the headboard adds texture and interest while also introducing colour.

2. In this grand Edwardian house, we created a sophisticated and calming retreat. A textured headboard with marble shelf sets the scene for the bed, while built-in lights negate the need for bedside tables. The fireplace was repaired and refurbished with new glazed tiles and a marble surround.

3. Sheer white curtains create an added softness to the master suite in James Street.

OTHER BEDROOMS

It's all about decorating when it comes to the remaining bedrooms in your home. These rooms are usually reserved for children, friends or when the in-laws come to stay. Think about what you need the space for and have fun with it. With the ability to layer textures and tones, use these spaces to play and experiment.

The joinery in these rooms should match their usage. We have several go-to's for kids' rooms, drawers being the ultimate when it comes to toy storage. Kids also love nooks, so window seats and secret rooms in roof spaces can be used for the win.

If you have spare bedrooms, you might like to turn one into a multipurpose space, such as a kids' playroom or study with a sofa bed for guests. When we design houses to sell, we ensure there is flexibility in the floorplan to appeal to different buyers. We do this by keeping the joinery flexible and ensuring that the colour palette is versatile enough for children and adults.

1. In this room, colour is incorporated in both the paintwork and the carpet, adding another dimension to the room.

2. Mixing new and old furnishings and layering a more sophisticated palette can add a level of chic to a child's retreat.

3. If you decide to paint the walls a neutral tone in multipurpose spaces, have fun with colour when it comes to furnishings to help bring the room to life.

Top Tip

Make your bedrooms playful but calming. If you can, create storage for toys so they are not all on display at once. It is much easier to rest if you are in a space that is free from clutter and chaos.

1. Have fun with your bedrooms, but think about how the room will be used over a period of time. This bedroom belongs to a young adult; it's fun and flexible and the styling does all the heavy lifting, meaning it can be easily changed once they leave home.

2. The second room is a toddler's and nursery room with a playful circular window. The curtains add a softness to the room, but again this is a flexible space that can change as the children grow.

2

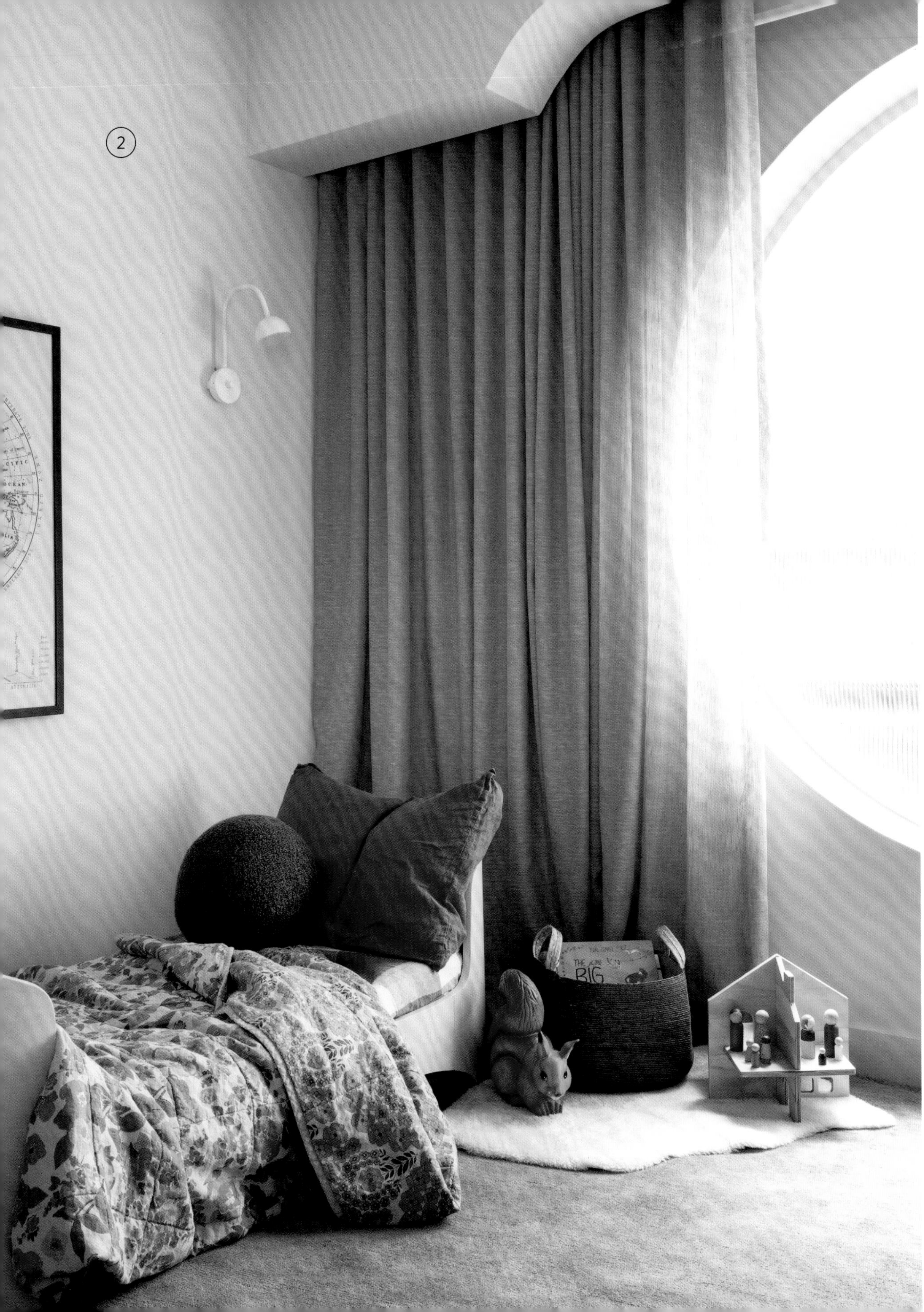

THE HOME OFFICE OR STUDY

In recent times, the home office or study has become an increasing necessity as more of us work from home. Planning an office can be fun and while you might not have the opportunity to design it from scratch, it is fairly easy to carve out a nook or adapt a multipurpose space to suit your office needs. Here are our top tips:

· Make a list of all the items you will need in your home office, then think about where they will go in your designated space. What storage will you need?

· Work out the best location for your office. If you are on the phone most days, you'll probably want a quiet space away from any noise. Alternatively, if clients are coming to your home, try to locate your office near an entry point so visitors aren't traipsing through the property.

· Understand the light. Will the sun shine directly on your computer screen at certain times of the day, causing screen glare? Try to set up your desk so it receives indirect light for the duration of your working hours.

· Think about ergonomics. Is your office chair the right height for your desk? Does it support your back, or would you be better off with a standing desk? Are cords and chargers within easy reach?

· Once you have set up your space, take a little time to style it. Collect three items you really love and put them on your desk. Think plants, cut foliage or flowers, photos or art.

· Finally, regularly declutter your office to keep it feeling fresh.

Top Tip

This is life-changing for some, but perhaps intuitive for others. Moving chargers and cords around the house or to and from work can be annoying. If you need to use your laptop in multiple locations, we recommend investing in additional cords, such as phone and laptop chargers, to save you having to set up and pack up each day.

LAUNDRIES & MUDROOMS

Laundries are often a room we spend a lot of time in, wishing we didn't have to! As they are used so regularly, thinking about the way this room will function best for you and your family can be really useful. Connect the laundry to the garage and, if possible, locate it in close proximity to the washing line, if one is available. Think about the interconnection of the butler's pantry, laundry and garage to help with tasks, such as bringing in the shopping and removing dirty shoes. Ideally, your laundry will house a trough, washing machine and/or dryer, storage/shelving and a space for laundry consumables and an ironing board/iron.

A mudroom is also fast becoming a favourite for families, as they provide a space to dump outdoor gear when we come inside. The mudroom, a term that comes from country living, now refers more to a utility area that takes clutter away from the entrance to our homes. Think coats, umbrellas, school bags, helmets, scooters, dog leads, work jackets, boots ... See if you can design practicality into your life by including a mudroom.

1. We all need clean clothes and few of us enjoy washing, so think about your ideal laundry set-up when you are planning out this space.

2. Bench space for folding and sorting clothes is a premium in laundries. If you have the luxury of a linen cupboard, then think about installing baskets for sorting dirty and clean washing.

CASE STUDY

COAL LANE

BUILDHER: STEPHANIE O'SULLIVAN
LOCATION: DUBLIN, IRELAND

What happens when an interior designer and architect are partners in life and in development? A refined process with spectacular results! Residing in beautiful (and chilly) Dublin, Stephanie and her husband, Graham, decided to apply their professional skills to improve their personal sphere. They had always dreamed of building their own home – to them, it simply made sense.

Encountering a challenging and expensive housing market while armed with discerning taste (thanks to their complementary careers), Stephanie and Graham were unable to find a home they liked in the location they wanted. After much searching and applying a little imagination, they eventually found a disused leather goods warehouse on a lane within their desired area. The wheels began to turn in motion for an industrial meets mid-century fluid two-bedroom home.

1

VISION

Inspired by the clever urban builds Stephanie and Graham encountered during their time in London, as well as the modernist work of Louis Kahn and Richard Neutra, the concept was for a home with strong lines and a feeling of grand scale, while still providing a homely environment for their children, all executed by a meeting of natural materials and light spaces. 'We wanted to ensure the design would support our family's needs but also be complementary to the industrial finish and concept. We didn't want the environment to feel too harsh given it was to be our family home, so we were conscious to minimise the number of colours and finishes, which has resulted in a very harmonious space.'

Envisioning a poured concrete finish inside and out set the tone for other materials. Choosing exposed concrete walls, ceilings and floors downstairs, as well as floors upstairs, the couple wanted some contrast on the upper level, so chose plywood panelling for the majority of the walls, with some painted in a plaster finish for balance.

For the bathrooms, Stephanie and Graham chose simple square mosaic tiles for the floors and walls. 'We wanted to create a clean contrast to the concrete, again keeping them nice and calm by only using one type of finish in each space.'

1. The poured concrete finish is repeated on the floor, walls and ceiling. Using a minimal palette helps to highlight the lovely furnishings.

2. A minimal façade in black is very striking. Here, the garage doors blend with the wall cladding.

3. The concrete staircase is a bold statement. Stephanie didn't need to install a handrail, but check local regulations in your area when designing this part of your property.

4. Full-height glazing and black doors are cleverly designed in replicated panels to give a seamless finish.

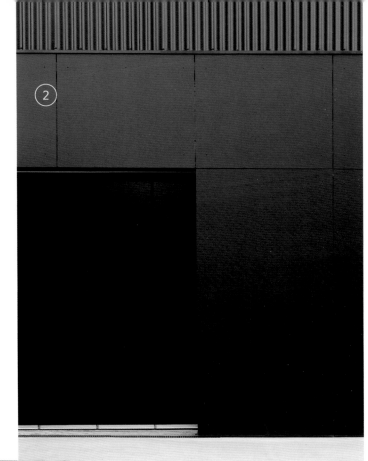

Playing to their skill sets, Stephanie says her role as the interior designer was to review Graham's plans and ensure that the interior layout maintained balance and flow.

For the most part it was smooth sailing for the family throughout most of their build, aside from the usual neighbourly objections (despite receiving full planning permission) causing only a minor delay to their timeframe.

The use of poured concrete did cause a little stress prior to execution. Unsure of how it would turn out due to the sheer volume being used and how its aesthetic might contribute to the finish and overall feel of the home, the couple knew it was a large risk, but Stephanie says it totally paid off. 'The cracks and flaws have turned out so beautifully that we feel it's been a big win. We love seeing the natural character of the concrete.'

As an active Instagram user, it felt only natural to document the journey of their build on a dedicated account – @coallanehouse – where the highs and lows of the build could be shared with those following along online, and which also led to a number of interviews with magazines, newspapers and radio stations.

RESULT

In a total transformation that remains true to the building's rustic industrial roots, the façade combines concrete, corrugated iron and original brick, while towering above, vast windows reflect the sky, at once adding a surreal modernist twist and harmony with the surroundings.

Indoors, character-rich concrete wraps the walls and floors, punctuated by floor-to-ceiling curtains, rich timber cabinetry and carefully placed windows and skylights.

'As the downstairs space is open plan and the kitchen is so prominent, the choice of timber was important. To bring in the mid-century aesthetic we love, we chose a sapele veneer with terrazzo and formica countertops. The warm nutty rust tones of the timber against the concrete works harmoniously.'

1. Large, custom-built joinery brings warmth to the space, and helps to separate the kitchen from the staircase.

2. The master bedroom is simply styled with a large plywood headboard with built-in lamps. The room overlooks one of the home's internal courtyards.

3. The terrazzo and formica benchtops in the kitchen tie the space together, providing a visual connection between the modern concrete and more traditional mid-century tones.

While the house has been constructed with two defined bedrooms, dual open-plan living spaces upstairs offer further opportunity to zone off bedrooms for guests, with future flexibility in mind throughout the 278m² (3000 ft²) space. 'Technically we have two static bedrooms (one upstairs and one downstairs), two flexible rooms upstairs, a laundry (with an enclosed outside terrace for air drying) and a large bathroom upstairs. Open-zone living downstairs comprises the kitchen, dining and living, plus two external courtyards, one of which is an extension of the internal living space.'

Stephanie says she loves the light and scale and effortless flow, particularly in the main open-plan living space, which offers access to the internal courtyard. 'It is so sheltered that we can even use it on days when the weather is changeable, which happens a lot in Ireland! I love stepping outside from the living room in the morning with a cup of tea – it's become a ritual. The amount of light in the house and our outside spaces have also turned out better than we expected. The process has been very enjoyable, which I believe comes down to our meticulous planning and level of detail prior to starting construction.'

Fabrics, such as these sheer curtains, can soften a space. Full-height windows with clean lines need to be considered early in the design phase, as they have structural implications for the property.

TIPS

Stephanie firmly believes that stress comes from lack of planning. 'Ensure that you have your interior design and finishes well and truly ticking along before you commence building, and consult an interior designer to ensure that you won't later be disappointed if a finish you have set your heart on is not possible due to the way the house is being built. This includes your heating system, built-in joinery and lighting plan. The more you plan, the less likely you will be disappointed.' That being said, in Stephanie's experience, more cosmetic choices can be edited and adapted later on. 'Don't be afraid to hold back on certain colour or decorative decisions until the space has been built – there is a lot to be said for realising how the space feels to understand what it needs.'

1. Stephanie spent time selecting the right materials for each part of the house. The upstairs rooms are clad with ply timber and minimally styled.

2. The staircase is positioned under large skylights, which bring light into the corridor and stairwell.

3. The bathroom is simple and functional with a free-standing bathtub and walk-in shower. A statement black radiator keeps the space warm in winter.

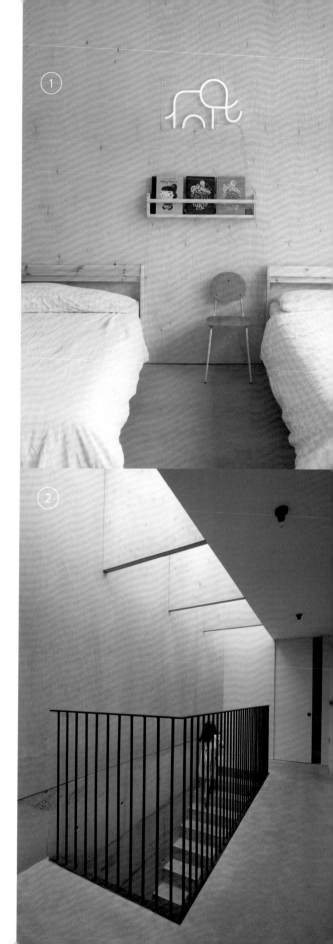

Setting her future sights on an old Irish country house, Stephanie is keen to make the most of Dublin while she waits for the right place to come up. 'Ireland has some incredible forgotten gems just waiting for a new lease on life!'

BUDGETS

MAKING A FINANCIAL INVESTMENT

Many people think that buying a run-down property and renovating it is the key to mega bucks. If only! Yes, you can make a profit from building and renovating, but on the flipside, if you're not careful you can end up sinking more money into a project that you no longer love. There are a few key elements to understand when buying a house, apartment or land to renovate or build on. Before you begin to venture down this path, it is really important to evaluate your value proposition.

Every time you build or renovate, ask yourself these questions:

· What problem am I trying to solve?
· Which of my core needs and wants am I trying to address?
· What result am I trying to achieve?

So often we encounter individuals who are planning renovations, deciding point blank that they need a large second storey with four bedrooms and two living rooms, pushing them to their financial limit. But when we really drill down to try and discover what they want to achieve and why, we realise that they haven't thought about it much at all. They are just doing what they think is right, presuming others do the same. Right? Maybe not!

When you're ready to make a significant financial investment, you need to ensure that your plans align with your needs and values. We have seen BuildHers scratch massive and expensive extensions and renovations, by asking them to simply examine these core areas. By doing this, they realised they could rework the space they already had and achieve a similar outcome (sometimes saving $750k along the way – true story!).

Before you make the leap, stop to think about your life plans. Are you going to live in the property long term? Once renovated, what will the property bring you that you can't buy in another? Will the change allow you to live your best life?

As corny as it sounds, we believe you can live the life that you dream and desire, and the only person who is in control and command of that life is you. So often we go along with other people's ideas and decisions without stopping to think about what is most important to us. Could the money you're investing in building or renovation be used to pursue other interests instead? Will a new home fulfil your dreams? If so, then go forth, but you need to be completely confident that the final outcome is worthy of the financial input.

After Kribashini and her partner discovered they were having a baby, their priorities changed and they decided to renovate their home in stages. The first step was to reconfigure the internal layout and install a new kitchen.

YOUR FUTURE

We are big believers in making sure that every large life decision we make moves our lifestyle and wealth forward. When we tackle a build or renovation, it must, in our eyes, move us towards better living (whatever form that may take) and a more fiscally secure future. It sounds boring but really and truly it's not! By simply running some numbers, you can establish if a renovation or new build makes financial sense, or if you are kissing goodbye to a pile of cash that could be better spent.

Building is also an investment in time (probably lots of it), and in our increasingly busy lives you want to ensure that expending this precious resource on your property is worthwhile for you.

1. Thinking about your future, along with the styles you love can be exciting but also daunting! Think about which design you want to commit to and ask yourself if it will stand the test of time.

    In this home we drew inspiration from mid-century architecture, which we have always loved. Because we want this home to be a long-term investment, we spent extra money on particular features, such as double-glazed steel windows and full-height brick walls.

2. Not every room needs to be unique, but adding a few key features can be a good way to maintain longevity of a space and create a home that really speaks to you.

DOES IT MAKE FINANCIAL SENSE?

Establishing the financial outcome of a build or renovation before you start is extremely important. Start by looking at your local market and assess the current value of your home. You can ask local real estate agents to value your property, but you can also do your own research to give you a better understanding of the market. Are there are any recently sold houses in a similar area? What did they sell for? Was it an easy or hard sale? Go and look at similar properties on the market – are they in a better or worse condition? Do they 'feel' better or are they in a better location? From this, work out a realistic sale price for your property.

Next up, estimate what your house will be worth after renovation. Create a brief concept plan and draw it out for your real estate agent, showing them some mood and materials boards (this will really help to paint the picture), and then ask them to forecast your home's future value.

Finally, you need to estimate your renovation, including rental costs if you need to live somewhere else during the works. Let's say you've budgeted $100k for your renovation, but the result will add $200k value to the property. Even if you run $10k over budget, you're still going to make $90k profit, making the renovation a worthwhile investment.

Now, what happens if you discover that the numbers don't add up and you're build or renovation is not going to result in a profit? You may decide that moving house is a better option, or you may conclude that staying where you are is more important than adding financial value to your home. That's totally fine! If you are staying and renovating what will be your dream home, then the trade-off may be worth it to you. It will really depend on your stage in life and what you want to achieve.

WHY THINGS COST WHAT THEY COST

When it comes to calculating the costs of building and renovating you need to consider two key elements: materials and labour. Materials make up the cost of what is being built: timber, stone, tiles; and labour is the cost of someone physically doing the work. It stands to reason that the longer something takes to build the more it will cost in labour. The more expensive the materials you choose, the more the overall cost will be. When you are building or renovating you are balancing thousands of hours of labour and hundreds, if not thousands, of individual components that have been welded, nailed, clamped, fixed, glued and screwed together to form your home. These items, tallied with the number of man hours (including profit for the person co-ordinating the job), is the cost of the works.

So, you can understand when someone asks, 'How much does it cost to build an extension with two bedrooms, a kitchen and a lounge?', that there is no correct answer to this question. It all depends on what materials you use and who you employ to do the job. Naturally, there are ranges of how much materials and labour can cost, and these ranges will vary depending on whether you are located in the country or in the city.

It is important to understand that budgets are broken incrementally over time. Every time you change or vary the works, it changes the overall cost. An $20/m^2$ here and $1,000 there can add up over a project, which is why a keen understanding of your costs from the beginning is imperative.

Top Tip

Plugging your numbers into a spreadsheet and understanding some of the broader costs can really help you gauge where you are headed and whether your project is viable. It will also help you to remember important items and prevent you feeling overwhelmed by all the variables.

Renovating traditional homes can be a minefield when it comes to calculating cost! The labour component can be especially difficult to estimate as you often uncover unexpected problems. Ensuring that you have a realistic handle on your budget and a good contingency plan will make this process much more enjoyable.

The Bayview house is a double-brick Edwardian home. This meant that changes to door openings and internal rooms were really going to add up. We needed to balance the potential cost of this change with the positive impact it would have on the space to determine if it was a worthwhile investment.

HOW MUCH IS A LOAF OF BREAD?

We love the 'how much is a loaf of bread?' analogy. When we buy a loaf of bread from the shops, its price may differ depending on where we buy it. It might cost $2 from the supermarket and $3 from the grocery store, but the convenience store might charge $4.95 for exactly the same loaf of bread.

Now let's say we wanted a fancy loaf of bread: artisan organic sourdough with a sprouted seven-seed mix. We are paying (and would expect to pay) a lot more for that bread. Building is the same. If you use base level materials from bigger stores that make those materials en masse, then you can save money, but if your values state that using bespoke materials is of utmost importance to you then your materials will be more expensive.

As a general rule, materials make up around 50 per cent of the build and we are left with around 50 per cent for labour, so you need to consider the complex interplay between these elements. How much time will it take to complete a particular job? How many stages and layers are there? How many people need to be involved? How many times do they need to come back to the site? How fiddly and precise is the work? Ornate work takes more time than standard work, for example, but minimalist work can also take longer as the job needs to be completed with more precision.

This is another way cost variations can creep into a job. If you have organised for work to be completed one way, and it becomes an unavoidably greater challenge, you can expect a variation. If you are managing the job yourself and you are paying people by the hour it is really important to be organised, as the hours add up. Knowing exactly when works need to happen throughout the process is important to streamline your schedule. This means being on top of what materials you need on site and when.

Top Tip

Hold fortnightly meetings with your team to pinpoint who is doing what in the coming weeks and beyond. If you haven't managed a project before or you don't have much construction knowledge, ask all the questions. Time is money, and it is worth your time to stay ahead of the trades to save that cash. This also helps to hold workers accountable when it comes to deadlines that they are setting for themselves.

CONTINGENCIES!

Unless you have a magic money tree, you will need to think ahead about how much your build or renovation is going to cost and whether you have this money available, or if you will need a loan. You should also think about contingency funds and a back-up plan.

Contingencies are vital for covering the what-ifs. What happens if you need more money to complete the works because you run over budget? What will you do if you get sick (think insurance here)? What if your family changes shape? Setting aside additional funds for unforeseen circumstances can lighten the load, and if you arrive at the end of your renovation without needing to spend this money then you have an absolute win on your hands.

Your mindset may be dictating the way you view things. If you are super optimistic, you may need to temper your optimism with a little realism. If you are cautious by nature, then you have probably already thought in this way. So often people start a build with no back-up plan and then get stuck purely because they fail to anticipate things going wrong – and when it comes to construction, projects tend to veer off course at least once.

Remember that your build or renovation has never been done before. This will be the first time that a specific set of trades builds to a specific set of plans in a specific location, and each of these elements pose a level of uncertainty and risk.

SOME MYTHS ABOUT COSTS IN THE BUILDING INDUSTRY

We meet many clients who have preconceived ideas about the building industry and its associated costs – not all of them positive! We would like to take this opportunity to dispel some of these myths.

EVERYONE IS TRYING TO TAKE ADVANTAGE OF YOU

This simply isn't true. Yes, there are some individuals who will try to maximise their profit or tell you things that are not true, but MOST tradespeople are trying to help. If you don't understand something, ask and do not be embarrassed. Building is simply the act of nailing, fixing, screwing and attaching one thing to another to make a house. So ask the questions until you understand the answers; just make sure you ask in a pleasant and respectful manner.

THERE IS A SECRET FORMULA THAT TELLS YOU HOW MUCH YOUR RENOVATION SHOULD COST

Unfortunately, there is no secret formula to help you calculate how much you should be spending. Every item you specify needs to be purchased, brought to site and assembled. There are just too many variables for a 'one cost fits all' approach. Having said that, there are standard ranges of rates that you can apply when mapping out your budget. Lean on the experience of your designer and/or builder where possible, and ask them to give you an approximate cost range.

BUILDERS ARE MAKING MASSIVE AMOUNTS OF MONEY

This is another myth. From a builder's perspective, running projects for clients is not the most lucrative job. While there are exceptions, most of the time builders work long hours on site from 7 am to 5 pm, seven days a week. Outside of these hours, they tender and quote on upcoming jobs and complete paperwork well into the night. If you think about all the elements a builder needs to organise and all the compliance they need to sign off, there is a lot of work to be done, and not without risk. This is what you are paying for when you hire a builder.

OWNER BUILDING WILL SAVE YOU HEAPS OF MONEY

It is true that taking on the role of owner builder may save you money, but it also may not. If you are organising the work, then you need to be available to co-ordinate the trades, order the materials and make sure everything happens when it should. You may also be charged more for trades. Builders often have established relationships with vetted trades and can reduce costs by buying bulk materials at cheaper rates. The time you spend tendering and organising will reap rewards in this area, but it won't necessarily cost you less.

COSTING
CONSTRUCTION

IT ALL ADDS UP

There are many misconceptions around determining how much your renovation will cost. This is by far the biggest challenge in the building and renovation process.

The industry can be complex. The aim of our initial engagement with most professionals is to figure out what we're doing, and how much it will cost. More often than not, we see people attacking their renovation themselves with a whole lot of gusto, and what feels like a bucketload of money! But in reality, they soon realise that those funds don't stretch far enough to achieve their objectives.

By establishing what's achievable (incorporating functionality and your personal values) and sourcing quotes along the way, you can figure out, with some degree of accuracy, the final cost of the proposed work and subsequently manage your project so it remains within budget.

Having said that, regardless of how much you plan ahead, you can still be caught out by a number of rogue factors. These might include:

· Renovating an older property
· Poor access to your home
· Varying levels on site requiring lots of cut and fill
· Poor soil conditions
· Structural issues requiring remediation
· Faulty wiring to be replaced
· Leaks and water damage
· Mold issues
· Code compliance issues
· Upgrades required to your mains services (sewer, water, power, gas).

If you're doing structural works, you are going to trigger more regulations, permits and approvals compared to what we call 'like-for-like renovation' without moving any walls.

Because existing properties don't necessarily match the way we want to live in our homes, the majority of renovations we see have structural implications, meaning you need to work alongside designers to help you design those walls, and organise the right documentation and approvals by your local authorities.

Restoration of period features, such as this
stained-glass window, can be mandatory if your
home is heritage listed. With so much charm and
beauty, they often complete a space but can add
significant cost to your renovation.

SO, HOW DO YOU GET THINGS COSTED?

Spreadsheets, we need spreadsheets! Who doesn't love a good spreadsheet? It's important to ensure you have enough money because you don't want to get caught out 70 per cent of the way through and realise you've run out of funds. This happens to an alarming amount of people, regardless of whether they are working with a set of professionals or not. Why? Because every time we build, we are creating something that wasn't there before, something that isn't just off the shelf. You are never going to manage the same project twice – and that's both a blessing and a curse!

Volume builders usually work on sites that have been meticulously costed, planned, rationalised or previously built. This means they have worked out all the kinks and are able to lower the cost. Unfortunately, when you are renovating your own home this isn't achievable.

You need a set of drawings or a scope document that describes the job. You should be clear with your design team about the construction budget and whose responsibility it is to design within those parameters (it's theirs). This should not be a set and forget type thing – the budget should be tested and checked at key phases of the design, including the concept stage, developed design stage and when quoting and tendering. The level of detail in your documents will always dictate the accuracy of these budget checks. It may be a square metre rate check or a simple conversation with your builder or designer, but the idea is to keep the budget at the front of everyone's mind and not get carried away. Budget-based value decisions should always be made in collaboration with you, if that is what you want. Remember it is your build, so ultimately you have the final say.

To help, you can employ a professional called a quantity surveyor (QS) or cost controller who can estimate the cost of building works. It's important to note that to employ a QS, you need a full set of design drawings and documents for them to cost labour and materials.

Alternatively, you can get quotes for the work yourself. During the design phase, there is time to do some groundwork sourcing quotes for big-ticket items. There are two ways that you can do this. The first is to hire a builder. The second is to work with tradespeople directly as an owner builder or self builder; however, to do this you need to understand any limitations imposed by your local governing body.

1. This gorgeous period fireplace and mantel complete the room. When sourcing quotes to restore original features, ask individual trades to come and inspect the work, as some tasks cannot be done in situ, which can affect your schedule and add cost.

2. This gorgeous full-height window looks seamless, but a lot of planning went into the structural design to achieve this aesthetic. If you like this look, show it to your team early so they can design it in.

3. Floating shelves are fantastic. If you think you might like to add a shelf in later, ask your builder or tradesperson to add additional support in the walls to avoid future costs.

4. If you can, set aside a healthy budget for furnishing. Being able to style your home with some drool-worthy pieces once the renovation is complete can be the icing on the cake!

①

OPTION 1: WORKING WITH A BUILDER

When you work with a builder, you need to accurately explain what the job entails. A lot of builders or contractors will look at a job and give you a quote. The less information you have to share about the job (drawings, specs etc.), the less reliable that quote will be. We really advise spending a little money on having your design documented and drawn by a professional, so the builder can visually see the scope of work, along with what they will be building and the associated costs of materials and labour. This document is also helpful for you to use as a 'line in the sand' for what should and shouldn't be included in a price. A builder will be able to give you professional advice, detailing whether the work can be completed within your budget.

It is up to you how much involvement you choose to have on your project. We often say you can pick and choose your path, but you can also pick and choose how little of that path you wish to be involved in. It is important to understand, however, that the less involvement you have in your design phase, the more likely it's not going to match the way you want to live in your home. You are the only person who knows how you want to live, and no matter how smart your design team are, they cannot read your mind nor understand your values, as they are specific to you.

Top Tip
Arrange site visits with your builder so that you have time to walk around and absorb the details and see how the finishes will come together.

1. Visit your site before wall finishes are applied to problem solve any potential issues.
2. Painting large swatch samples allows you to view their colour at different times of the day.
3. Your builder will have a wealth of knowledge, so feel comfortable asking how exposed materials will be finished or how they will look when butted up against another material.

OPTION 2: WORKING AS AN OWNER BUILDER

In this option, you assume the role of the owner builder (project manager) and work directly with trades or subcontractors. Depending on how much of the design work you've undertaken yourself, you may or may not have detailed drawings to rely upon when engaging trades. We recommend that, at the very least, you have a conceptual floorplan worked up to help guide your conversations with individual trades. Drawings are the easiest way to communicate what you want to achieve, and even if you only have a set of conceptualisations without a set of elevations (vertical plans), this can still be helpful in guiding their understanding.

If you are looking to manage your plasterer, tiler, electrician and other trades on your own, you'll need to coordinate them individually. Based on the costs, some works will require a contract (there are varying cost points in different countries that will determine this, so touch base with your local government who can advise you on building regulations and protocols).

Ideally, you want to source prices before you start. Because you're not working with a builder who will give you a total price straight up, you will need to collate the quotes that come in from all the tradespeople you are going to use. You will then need to work with them in tandem. They know how to work together, and more often than not these roles are coordinated by a builder, but if you are project managing the construction yourself, you are going to have to take on this role. Finding people that suit your personality and style of working is key here.

Tote Tips
We love being on site and seeing our vision come to life. Don't be afraid to embrace your renovation – it's so much fun seeing your new home take shape.

1. As an owner builder, you can structure your project so that a qualified carpenter manages the day to day on site, leaving you to focus on the design and quoting.

2. Sometimes we fall in love with a particular design feature after renovation commences. If this happens, weigh up the cost benefit and its value to you.

3. Measure twice, cut once!

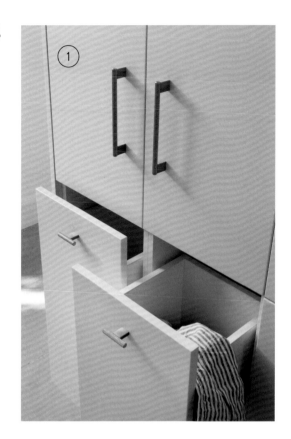

MY BUDGET AND COSTS DON'T MATCH!

This happens a lot, because until we actually start designing we don't realise what we want to do. When we see images of what we like and what we want, we don't have a concept of related cost. Part of the reason for this is the unknown price of labour.

It's really easy to go shopping and pick your fixtures, vanities, finishes, tap wear and mirrors; they're pieces we can pick in a store or an online shop. But what happens when quotes from builders and trades come in over budget?

The truth is that sometimes we cannot afford what we want to do, and the reality of the situation is to go back and reassess the work required – or find more money.

IF WE CAN'T ABRACADABRA MORE MONEY, WHAT DO WE DO?

We need to revisit our design! The biggest impact you can make to cut costs is to look at your floorplan and reduce its size. Sometimes we dream really, big right? There's nothing wrong with that! We start designing our homes in the hope that we'll achieve our dream, so we tend to design as big as we possibly can, but every square metre we add to a floorplan adds to our cost. That's the real challenge.

WHAT HAPPENS WHEN WE CANNOT REDUCE OUR FLOORPLAN?

If this happens, then you will need to start looking at fixtures and finishes, along with the finish of the house, its style and the complexity of the design. This might include the number of crevasses, high roofs and/or specifications of the windows, as well as whether you have a substantial amount of work to do to bring your home up to scratch.

1. Using a pre-finished melamine joinery material for an internal carcass can save costs, as you don't need the inside to be laminated or painted.

2. Feature lighting can make a big impact, but it doesn't need to be in every room. Make a single statement with a light you love and balance out the budget.

3. A fun and inexpensive hack is to paint IKEA bunk beds in a bold colour.

OUR COST-SAVING TIPS

DO MORE YOURSELF

Outside of DIY, there are many things you can do to save money on your project, such as obtaining technical reports yourself instead of hiring designers or architects to do this, or chasing or following up on quotes and gathering information. If you do decide to work with an architect, negotiate to take on some on the interiors work yourself, or liaise directly with the builder (and interior designer) to help pull these together.

TAKE ON THE CONTRACT ADMINISTRATION OF YOUR BUILD

Rather than asking your architect or designer to administer your building contract, you can manage your builder directly. You can pay invoices and directly negotiate problems that arise. If you are working with a builder who is giving you a fixed-price contract and managing all aspects of the build, this is a little trickier to do. Some builders might be willing to allow you to do more yourself, thus saving you costs.

DELIVERY MODEL

Figure out early on if your chosen design and building delivery model is right for your budget. Can you afford to hire a bespoke builder or project manager, or are you better off managing the project yourself? Your delivery model will heavily influence cost, so if your budget is at the lower end and you're working with a high-end architect, it's going to be a real challenge to align the two. Choosing your delivery model early can end up saving you thousands of dollars and heartache.

EARLY BUILDER ENGAGEMENT

Regardless of whether you hire a builder to manage your project or you decide to manage the trades directly, it's useful to involve invested parties early on in the design process. This might involve a working session with individuals to ascertain where key or potentially hidden costs may lie, and, importantly, where you might be able to reduce costs. To have these conversations you will need an architect or draftsperson to draw up the plans for you. Alternatively, you can ask a builder come through your home to help you identify where costs may blow out.

1. DIY shelving is a great option if you're looking for ways to save money. These shelves were made from recycled timber and paired with simple brackets from the hardware store.

2. Implementing small cost savings here and there adds up over the course of a project. Carpeting only two-thirds of a staircase is a neat trick that can save money.

3. If you feel confident, have a go at painting and styling rooms yourself. Decorating a child's bedroom can be fun without the stress that can come with styling a larger space.

4. This walk-in robe is perfectly suited to the master suite. Consider what level of finish is appropriate for each room.

DON'T RULE OUT CHANGE

Do you have to extend or can you restructure your existing floorplan to accommodate your needs? Often, we hear people wanting to extend before realising the cost of the extension, and instead find a way to make their renovation work within their current footprint.

BUILD IN STAGES AND DIY!

If you're limited in funds or capacity, another option is to complete your renovation in stages. Identify the key areas that you want to change and then start with the kitchen, then the bathroom and so on. Keep in mind that you need to have a master plan (see page 72) to make sure you're not going to do anything that will impact further changes down the line. You could save even more by taking on elements, such as painting and landscaping, yourself. A little DIY never hurt anyone! You will learn something new and you might even enjoy it!

REDUCE THE EXTENT OF YOUR BESPOKE JOINERY

Bespoke joinery and cabinetry for kitchens, storage cupboards and robes can dramatically increase your costs depending on their style and finish. If you run into budget problems, look at cheaper off-the-shelf options that will give the same or similar desired effect.

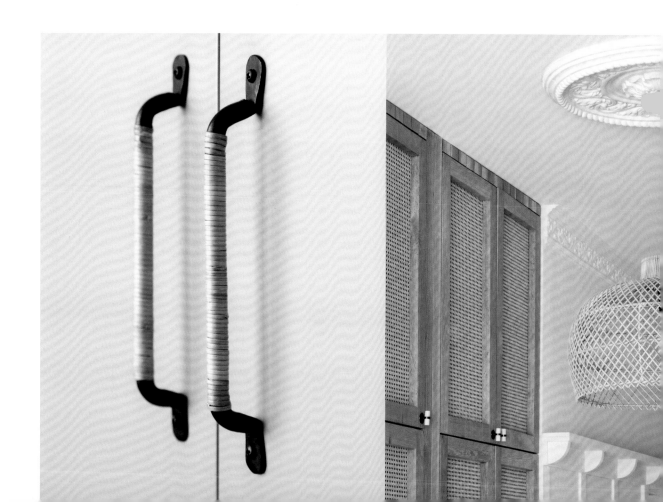

BUY YOUR OWN FIXTURES AND FITTINGS

Shopping around for your own fixtures and fittings can save you money. You can often buy lights, taps, handles, doorknobs etc. in bulk from online stores. Try to buy the best quality you can afford: apart from getting a heavy workout, these are items you will touch and feel every day.

DON'T SKIMP ON HEATING AND COOLING

Think long term when it comes to heating and cooling. The thermal properties of our homes are super important, particularly through Australian summers! If you build your envelope well, you can incorporate a more sustainable home that will reduce the future cost of bills and utilities.

TIME FOR A REASSESSMENT?

If your project is still coming in over budget and you cannot work out a way to pull it back, it's time to take a pause. You might like to reconsider if you should stay in your home or move to a new property. Although this may feel like you're taking 10 steps back after deciding to renovate, it might still be the best solution in order to achieve your goals.

Cabinetry handles can be purchased from a builder or joiner/cabinet maker, or you can source them yourself. They can add a bespoke feel to your home.

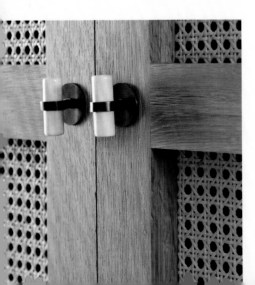

CASE STUDY

AFTER HOURS FARM

BUILDHER: SAMANTHA SUTTON
LOCATION: MICHIGAN, USA

It's not very often that a house flagged for demolition finds its saviour. Finding the US property market unaffordable, when Sam started looking for a home she knew it needed to be something unique. Spotting an abandoned, boarded-up farmhouse outside her home town in Michigan, Sam was intrigued. In a small town, it didn't take long to find the farmer who owned the old home.

Taking a year and a half to close due to the lengthy process of converting the land from agricultural to residential zoning, Sam and partner Sean bought the 160-year-old farmhouse for $26,000 in 2018.

VISION

The first time Sam and Sean gained access to the property, they found it had become the neighbourhood party house. Graffitied and trashed, the house was full of beer bottles, with all the boarded-up windows smashed in. But Sean (who studied architecture) recognised the potential offered by the relative soundness of the floors, walls and structure – regardless of the questionable aesthetic state of repair! The bones were promising.

In an homage to the traditional residential buildings of her home town and the roots of the farmhouse, Sam wanted to keep as much of the property's original aesthetic as she could. 'The overall design goal of the house was to keep a timeless, lived-in feel, while updating the interior with modern amenities. We wanted the exterior to look exactly like it did 160 years ago with white-wood siding and a stone skirt. The interior will make use of the classical architecture, but with a modern floorplan, natural woods, marble and cream-white finishes.'

Taking on such a large project, Sam has found that tackling one room at a time has made the process digestible. 'I've been using mood boards to see how different design elements work together visually. I started with the exterior, then moved on to the mudroom, each bathroom and so on.'

The old home was relocated to its new site – a huge undertaking that was definitely a labour of love. Here, the house sits on supports ready to be restored.

JOURNEY

The worst part of the house was the crumbling 1.5 metre (5 ft) deep basement. After some deliberation, Sam and Sean concluded that the cost of repairing the basement would be the same as moving the whole house and digging down to build a full-height basement – so they dug a new basement 9 metres (30 ft) back on the block, and moved the whole house on top!

Having worked in commercial roofing for five years, Sam was comfortable working with different trades, feeling very lucky to have a super flexible team to work with. Anything Sam doesn't know, her contractors are willing to help her figure out.

Once the house was moved into place, Sam and Sean got to work, with a rough idea of which jobs they would outsource, and what they would complete themselves. With an initial budget of around $400,000, as they worked through the process of the build and identified where they might want to upgrade their materials (e.g. wider plank floors and more expensive tiles), Sam got to work offsetting costs, and saved on labour by tiling herself.

Sam and Sean's first challenge was moving back into her parents' basement down the road for the length of the build, requiring a certain amount of adjustment! The second challenge was realising how much of the house would need to be changed to meet current-day codes. This meant replacing floor joints, the roof and further details that had not been accounted for in the budget. The third great challenge for the couple was 2020's lowlight – Covid-19.

As the couple reached the halfway point of their build, the world slowed down. Their trades paused work at the end of March, right at the point of installing the dry walls and insulation. The couple managed to keep the ball rolling where they could, completing some painting, tiling and roofing themselves. Production of materials also ground to a halt, meaning a large amount of necessary materials were put on back order.

Initially hoping for a June completion, Sam and Sean are now looking at a move-in date in July. Forced to slow down their process, the couple are taking it day by day as materials become available once again, and the final stages of the build are completed by specialised trades.

(SO FAR)

As they watch the reinstallation of the walls, Sam loves seeing her sketches come to life.

Adding a master bedroom to the second storey, the couple had originally planned to make the home a four-bedroom house, but in the end they decided to sacrifice the fourth bedroom to create a master en suite.

Wrapped in six giant windows, a huge clawfoot bathtub overlooks the gorgeous view at the back of the property. Hills lead to a small stream where fawns and other wildlife can be spotted grazing and drinking – one of the reasons the couple fell in love with the property in the first place. If all continues to go to plan, they should come in just under budget!

When you strip back the wall lining you are left with a beautiful skeleton ready to be re-wired, plumbed, insulated and given a whole new lease on life.

TIPS

Throughout the chaotic and often stressful process of trying to renovate during a pandemic, Sam took comfort in the BuildHer community, reminding herself daily that she was not alone. She tells us, 'It's nice to know there's a whole community of crazy-minded, driven females out there!'

Sam's advice is to go for it – all in! 'I know I initially had some reservations and thought, will I be able to do this, design something like you see online? You second-guess yourself – will I be good enough to pull it off? But once you dive in, you'll do it and you'll be able to make it yours.

'Don't get discouraged. You'll figure it out. It made our relationship stronger – if one of us is having a bad day the other says, "Look how far we've come, not much more to go. There is light at the end of the tunnel!"'

It's so often the power of hindsight that helps you realise just how large a project can become. Sam says of the process, 'To be in there and see it completed and all coming back to life, becoming a liveable space, is super rewarding. I love it, I want to do more! But maybe not as intense.'

1

WHAT'S NEXT

Taking such a deep dive into her own project has made Sam realise she would love to help others do the same. When you feel like you've hit and resolved every possible speed bump along the way, you're left with considerable wisdom!

1. With a classic colour palette of white weatherboards and black trims, the exterior of the farmhouse has a timeless aesthetic.

2. Having progressed leaps and bounds, the exterior is now painted and a three-car garage adds contrasting scale while complementing the main house.

CONSTRUCTION

READY, SET, BUILD!

You've planned, you've designed, you've sourced your team. The time has finally come to lay down those foundations or start tearing down walls. So jump in, have as much fun as you can and enjoy the journey! Helping to shape spaces and watch them come to life with a design and materials that you've chosen can be genuinely thrilling. So, why not make the most of it? You might just become addicts like us!

In addition, by fostering meaningful relationships with your team, you will not only make the process easier for everyone concerned, but you'll learn new skills from your tradespeople along the way. And if you get on well with your individual contractors, you'll be more inclined to use them on your next project. Networks are everything!

As we've discussed, there are generally two types of construction when it comes to building and renovating: building on an empty site, and extending or adding to an existing building.

BUILDING FROM SCRATCH

STAGE ONE: IN GROUNDS AND FOUNDATION

This is where in-ground services are put (believe it or not) in the ground, along with the footings and substructure. This might be a concrete foundation or concrete stumps with a raised timber floor. The services – plumbing, electrical and/or gas – will run either in the ground or under the floor.

STAGE TWO: FRAME AND LOCK-UP

This is when our structural steel or timber frame is built, including the external and internal walls, as well as the roof structure, roof lining and external windows and doors. Lock-up means that the structure is watertight and secure.

1. Different plaster finishes are used for painting, wallpapering and tiling. The surrounds of these doors are being prepped for a paint finish.

2. Once the frame is up, you can suddenly feel the size of the rooms. Cables and pipes run inside the walls which will connect to your switches, taps, toilets and sinks.

3. Once the insulation has been laid out, then the plasterboard linings can be installed and the joints stopped. When you start closing up the walls, it begins to feel like a home to be!

STAGE THREE: FITOUT AND ROUGH-INS

By this stage the building really feels like it's coming together! Insulation and in-wall services, such as power, water, gas and data (internet), are installed and internal walls are plastered. Each service needs to be brought through the wall where a connection or outlet is required.

STAGE FOUR: FINISHING

Now this is when it gets really exciting! All those finicky decisions you've made along the way now come to fruition. Finishing includes laying floors, painting, wallpapering, affixing joinery, cabinetry, sinks, taps, appliances, the list goes on! This is when your building site becomes a home.

BUILDING OR RENOVATING ON AN EXISTING SITE

Outlining the build and renovation stages for an existing property is hard to define because each project is unique. Sometimes it is just a renovation within existing external walls, but this becomes more complex if you extend out or up, as you are essentially building and renovating at the same time. If you are extending, then the general process is the same as building from scratch, but your first step will be to organise demolition of any redundant walls that are not needed in the new design, ensuring that the existing structure is propped up to support its weight. If you are renovating within existing external walls, then the process usually starts at stage three after any internal walls have been demolished.

1. It's important to look at material swatches in daylight, as well as under artificial light, as the tone and overall feel of a material can change in different lighting conditions.

2. Wiring and cabling will be pulled through the walls after the plasterboard is installed. The wires will normally be extra long and then cut to size, to avoid any issues with connections.

3. Take your tile samples to site to establish how you will detail around features, such as this in-wall recess.

4. Moving materials around and out of the way is a constant, especially if you are working in a tight space or living in your renovation.

LIVING IN THE RENO

Living on site during construction can be stressful and exhausting, but many of us don't have the luxury of residing elsewhere. Here we look at why many of us choose to 'live in the reno', along with our BuildHer tips for construction survival!

WHY DO WE LIVE ON SITE?

TO SAVE MONEY

Rent is expensive! If you're going to rent a property for the duration of your build then it makes sense to live locally, but depending on your suburb rental prices may be high. Factor in your mortgage AND the cost of your build or renovation, and it can suddenly become financially impossible. By living on site, the money you save in rent can be put towards finishes such as joinery or furnishings.

TO MONITOR THE PROJECT

By living on site, you know when tradespeople are coming and going, how the team is working together and if something is not quite right. Being on site can solve countless issues, because of the inherent sense of accountability that builders, contractors or trades will feel working alongside you.

TO FIELD QUESTIONS

It's much easier (and faster) to answer those pesky questions that crop up along the way if you are always available. Conversely, you will quickly spot elements that don't adhere to your plans, such as incorrectly placed walls and windows, and be able to immediately follow up.

TO SAVE TIME

Not an obvious one, but regular travel to and from your site is time consuming. Let's say the site is 30 minutes from where you live, so that's an hour round trip every time you visit. We would normally want to be on site at least twice a week (it's too exciting not to be!), to monitor progress and ask questions. You also need to time your visits to coincide with relevant trades, which is less convenient.

THEFT

It's sad that this is a consideration, but it is a prevalent issue. Building sites are often broken into by opportunists, and by living on site you will serve as a deterrent.

THE CONS

We'll be honest, it's not comfortable. Often there's a big hole (or several big holes) in the wall where hot and cold air can get in, making things unpleasant depending on the season. Most renovations involve the kitchen and perhaps the bathroom, which can be inconvenient at the best of times. Endless takeaways and showering at work or a friend's house can take its toll. Additionally, services might be temporarily severed while wiring or plumbing is completed.

Privacy is also an issue, as there is no escape when you are living on a building site. People come and go from early morning until late afternoon, which can be disruptive and overwhelming, especially if you are introverted by nature.

1. This build is still in the framing stage. The scaffolding provides access to the upper floors and will remain in place until the external cladding is completed.

2. Being able to shut out your renovation from time to time is important, not just for privacy but for your own sanity!

Speaking of introversion, your personality type is also key. Are you someone who can roll with the punches and deal with less-than-ideal living conditions, or do you need things just so? Everyone has their limits and there is no right or wrong, but being realistic from the outset about what you're prepared to put up with is important. Some people love camping; others couldn't think of anything worse ...

Did we also tell you about the never-ending stream of dust and dirt? You might have duct-taped all the gaps, but dust will ALWAYS find a way in! This might be mildly annoying to you or send you into a fit of continuous cleaning for the duration of the project.

Finally, it is important to check that you are allowed to live in the building during particular stages of renovation. Your insurance may be affected, so you'll need to ensure that you remain covered.

KRIBASHINI'S TOP TIPS:

· Make sure you're in the right headspace for your renovation. Don't feel rushed or pressured by trades or designers into making quick decisions.

· If you can afford it, hire a storage container to store any furniture you don't need, to create more space for tradespeople moving through the property.

· If you can, keep one room separated from the works and set up a heated, clean, dust-free sanctuary. This is especially important if parts of the property are open to the elements for a time.

· Designate a spot for building debris and rubbish.

· If you are renovating in stages, try and plan it logically so that you can work your way through the site and not go back on yourself.

· Speak openly about your renovation at work and try to negotiate reduced hours or working from home. Take annual leave on key days, so that you can be there when you need to.

· Hold regular meaningful and documented meetings with your trades/builders to avoid having to answer potentially big questions when you're running out the door and don't have time to properly think about the answer.

· Set up a temporary kitchen somewhere with hot water plumbed in. Keep clean kitchen equipment, such as saucepans, dishes and cutlery, in a sealed plastic tub to prevent dust getting in.

1. Take the time to get used to your renovation. Walk around the site and try to be at peace with the mess!

2. If you are managing trades directly, spending your weekends cleaning up will become a regular pastime. Set up a bin and refuse area to avoid rubbish being discarded everywhere.

REBEKA'S TOP TIPS:

· Do whatever you can to prepare for dust. Try to block up the entry to the renovation as best you can and seal the openings. This may not be convenient if you want to constantly keep an eye on progress, but it will give you and your family some privacy and help keep the renovation where it is meant to be.

· Remind yourself why you are living the way you are and keep an eye on the end result (it will help when things get frustrating). Be prepared to spend a small fortune on takeaway!

· Pack up everything you don't need. For example, if you are renovating in summer, pack away your winter clothing.

· A shoes-off rule will really help! Outside there might be mud and mess, which is very easily walked into the house.

· Demarcate the renovation into zones and think about what you need to do and when. Completing an *en suite* before the rest of the works, for example, will give you access to a bathroom, but it can also mean living in the renovation for longer.

· Finally, have a sense of humour! In the grand scheme of things, the disruption will only last for a short period of time and the end result will feel even more luxurious and lovely after a little bit of 'camping' in your own home.

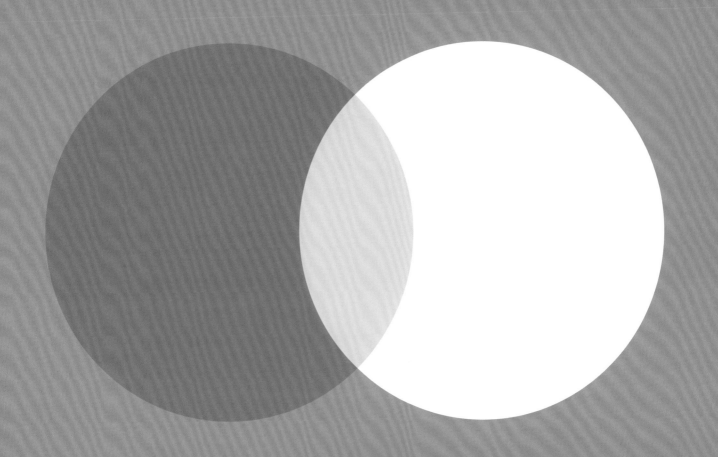

QUOTES
& TENDERS

THE IMPORTANCE OF QUOTES

Obtaining quotes is one of the best ways to ensure that we're getting value for money. To be fair, we're all pretty good at shopping around! Quotes and tenders set the baseline of cost control for each service and, in many ways, provide your first insight into what a working relationship with that trade or builder will look like. Their initial communication and service style will help you assess whether they are a good personality fit, and how the works might be managed if you choose to give them the job. If you start off on the wrong foot, then you will probably look elsewhere; alternatively, it could be the beginning of a fantastic working relationship!

Sometimes we hear from women who are concerned they've accepted a quote or tender with myriad terms and conditions, but have no problems and a great experience. Others receive quotes that are vague and then end up getting burned: in part due to not understanding what's been quoted, but also because they don't realise the extent of the job and haven't assessed if the quote is competitive or comparable.

You might be surprised to hear that quoting is more than just dollars. It also extends to your values, because building is a journey that involves managing relationships with different personalities to bring this chaotic world together. At the end you have a building, whether that's a house, apartment, condo or a small shed in the garden. Whatever it may be, you need to pull together resources, people, materials and skills to achieve the finished product.

WHAT'S THE DIFFERENCE BETWEEN A QUOTE AND A TENDER?

A tender is simply a formal term for a quote. It is usually reserved for big-ticket items such as construction. A quote is used for smaller jobs that cost as little as $200 and up to $150k, while we tender for more expensive services, usually from $150k to a million-plus dollars.

You can ask someone to tender to you for works and services. This means that you're asking them to review the work required and then give you a price for delivering that work. There's some really handy information out there, and we've got some great tips to help you through the process in a meaningful and policy-driven way.

1. Consider your skirting detail early on in the design. Here a simple neat hardwood skirting has been painted.

2. Small details, such as a square-set ceiling or the need for a bulkhead, are sometimes overlooked or unclarified by an inexperienced renovator, leading to unexpected additional costs.

HOW TO SOURCE QUOTES & TENDERS

Whenever we source a quote or tender, we want to make sure we receive up to three quotes for each service. On occasion, there may be reasons for only obtaining one price, but when we do that it means we don't truly know the market value of that item.

There are challenges to sourcing quotes and tenders because you're asking contractors or subcontractors to invest time they often don't have putting together a quote for you. We highly recommend starting this process as early as possible. Quite often, if we want to get three prices, we initially contact six contractors or sub-contractors to see if they are interested. This will depend on the complexity of the job and your budget.

1

1. In a new build, architects or designers and engineers will create separate drawings and plans for the builder to follow, so it's important to coordinate these in a timely fashion. In this home, the striking structural steel frame became a design feature in its own right.

2. Similarly, fireplaces require certain fire-safe materials to be placed prior to installation. If done correctly, a modern fireplace can be a beautiful feature in a home.

UNDERSTAND THE PRODUCTS BEING QUOTED

It is important to have a good understanding of the type of work each person delivers. Whether you're employing an architect, draftsperson or a building surveyor, you need to know the ins and outs of what they do, and how they fit within the framework of your build.

A good example is working with architects. It is not unusual to encounter a mismatch between your budget and the price of products an architect might choose to use. If that architect is operating in a high-end sphere, your budget won't align and there will be a disconnect from the start. You want to find an architect that is capable (and willing) to work within your realm and know that their products and services speak directly to you. Most architects will say they can respond to your vision and provide you with a design that meets it, but they all have their own signature aesthetic. Of course there will be variances in their work, but you should be able to see a clear design theme as well.

In contrast, often when we look at builders' works there is a larger variation because they are building what is documented, and what has been designed. They could be building a Hampton-style home for one client at the same time as someone who is seeking a modern, sleek look.

BE EXPLICIT

In order to assist those who will work on your project, it's important to clearly define the job at hand and identify all the stages that you want them to be involved in. Understanding a little about each of the trades will help you put together the scope of the job (check out our glossary on page 282 for a breakdown of who does what).

For example, if you're asking for a quote from a carpenter, you want to make sure that you've identified every piece of carpentry work required across the entire job or, if you're not sure, that you discuss the project with them so they can help you understand what's required, along with how many trips to site they'll need to make.

Being clear about what you're asking for is really important. We recommend writing a document that explains the scope of the work. This could be in the form of drawings, documentation and/or specs. You also want to provide an expected start date and realistic timeframe of how long the job will take. This helps tradespeople plan their workload and schedules. They may come back to you and explain that they're busy at certain points of your build, but this open dialogue and transparency will help you better negotiate a successful outcome for everyone, whoever you're dealing with. This level of discussion is also vital for longer-term relationships, such as a builder who might be managing all the works for you.

When managing trades directly, you need to be more prescriptive as you are managing a chain of works in progress. This often means that you can't push back works to suit their timeframes, as they need to be available when it suits your schedule. For this to happen, you need to know (within reason) their future availability prior to the work.

Top Tip

Always try to remain one step ahead. There are lead trades that you need to procure early because they will work with you throughout the entire process. There's no point trying to source a quote the week before the work is due to start, because you're going to put pressure on the individual to move jobs around to fit yours in. As a result, their prices might escalate because they need to mobilise quickly and source materials at short notice. Aim to source quotes at least two months ahead of construction and factor in long lead times for big-ticket items, such as steel, joinery and windows. Planning ahead will also give you time to establish if you need permits. Once you've sourced quotes and you're waiting for the work to start, use this time to look at your finances and work through the costs and planning steps required to successfully manage your project.

The Alpha house kitchen incorporates a simple and elegant design. Important details to convey to your design team might include pattern matching if using a stone benchtop, finishes on timber battens or the look and feel of open shelving.

OUR TOP TIPS FOR ACCURATE QUOTING

· Put together a request for quotation or tender document. This paperwork describes the job that you are asking to be priced. For example, it should detail what you are supplying, along with what you're asking the contractor to provide. It may also determine the schedule and any delay costs.

· Establish if the quote is estimated by a rate or by labour and materials. For example, a caulker may quote you $4,000 for labour and materials, or they could charge you $10 per linear metre, which may comprise 20 metres (65 ft) of work. This is known as a linear rate.

· Consider a contract. If you want special conditions or terms, you may need to hire a lawyer to draft the documentation. If you are hiring a custom builder or design build team, they will have a contract for you to sign. You must understand the terms and conditions you are agreeing to, so read carefully!

· Don't rush. Try to give potential contractors between four and six weeks to provide you with a quote. You want to ensure that you give all of your builders and/or contractors an appropriate amount of time to quote on the job. Try to send out your documents on the same day and clearly state the day you would like them returned. During this time, a builder may ask for more information. If they do, proper process dictates that all builders should receive the same answer regardless of whether they asked the question or not.

1. In case of high ceilings, contractors will often ask to visit a site or home prior to quoting, to ensure they include pricing for necessary access equipment or scaffolding.
2. Floating shelving can require a fixing in the wall – be sure to flag this with your trade if this is what you want.

· Compare quotes. Once you receive your quotes, it's time to review and tabulate them in a spreadsheet. This not only enables you to compare pricing, but also ensures that builders and/or contractors have priced the same drawings and products, and allowed for the same inclusions and exclusions across the project.

· Consider height and access. If work is required at heights above 2 metres (6.5 ft), such as painting ceilings, installing gutters or roof work, you need to ensure that your contractors include the cost of elevated work platforms, scaffolding or access equipment in their quote. Alternatively, if you choose to provide this equipment, make sure your contractors don't include these items in their overall price.

· Always ask for copies of insurance and warranties once the works are complete, as well as making sure that everyone has their registrations and licences in place prior to starting your job.

· Lastly, many quotes stipulate it is your responsibility to move necessary furniture for clear access. For example, a painter will require you to move items away from the walls before starting work.

HOW TO BUILD GOOD WORKING RELATIONSHIPS

Do you ever hear stories about relationships with tradespeople or building contractors turning sour? We hear about them far too often, and it's a shame they receive more attention than the good news stories. There are many reasons why relationships between invested parties break down, and we can 100 per cent confirm that there are always two sides to the story.

Creating and fostering a good relationship with your builder, architect or tradesperson is important, but it's also rewarding, especially if you want to enjoy your building journey. Builders typically gain reputation through word of mouth, so it's in their best interest to complete a job to the best of their ability and communicate with you at all stages of the build.

When it comes to choosing a builder, it's a jungle out there. There are young and old builders, those with lots of experience dealing and communicating with clients and those who haven't had that experience and are learning as they go. The first step is to find a builder who not only comes recommended, but is also the right personality fit for you. They should have good communication skills and a respect for what you're trying to achieve and why. They also need to suit your style of working and understand your values.

Top Tip

If a builder fails to communicate well during the quoting stage and you have reservations about giving them the job, rather than discounting them altogether, it might be worth having a frank conversation about your concerns and see if you can find a way to better communicate before making a decision.

1. An organised builder is a good sign! This contractor kept all their documents and plans in sealed boxes – nice!

2. Before any tiles are laid, walk through your renovation with your builder – this is a great time to fix any last errors before final work commences.

SET CLEAR EXPECTATIONS

· When you are upfront with a builder, you help them understand what is important and potentially non-negotiable for you. An example of this might be the need for a fixed completion date. Perhaps you're renting a home for the duration of the works and the end date of your rental needs to coincide with the completion of your renovation. There are clauses in contracts that deal with this, but we want to build a good relationship and only refer to contracts if and when we have to.

· When you're talking to contractors about problems, do so in an informed way. Set a meeting time and write an agenda so everyone knows what will be discussed. Take notes and circulate them after the meeting. Make sure you write down who's responsible for following up something and when it needs to be done by. The clearer you can make this the better, and the more decisions you can make together will help you and/or your builder better manage the project.

· Be cautious about making design changes, as they can lead to delays and mistakes.

· Visit the site regularly and be informed about what's coming up. Ask questions that are open-ended to foster good discussions. Don't micro-manage and do show that you trust all relevant parties to complete the works within your expectations and without shifting the goalposts along the way.

· Being part of an online community, such as BuildHer, can be really helpful. Building can be lonely! Sometimes you might feel like it's you against an entire team of professionals who are more informed and that your opinions mean less, which isn't right. Connecting with others who are going through the same process enables you to share problems and receive help, guidance, advice and confidence, as well as manage any small insecurities that might pop up.

· Lastly, address bad behaviour upfront. If your project has started and all of a sudden your builder is not playing by the rules you agreed to, it's important to address that behaviour straight away. Being dismissive, putting on a show to his or her peers, or ignoring you on site is not on. This should be cleared up immediately in the hope of forging a clear and honest building journey together.

CASE STUDY

THE ARMADALE HOUSE

BUILDHER: IVY HUANG

LOCATION: MELBOURNE, AUSTRALIA

TIMING

VISION

CHALLENGES

RESULT

TIPS

WHAT'S NEXT

Ivy Huang and her partner, Adrian, were on the hunt for a family home. Finding the Melbourne property market for family homes within their budget disappointing, Ivy changed strategy, and was won over by a 1910 Edwardian weatherboard cottage with great bones, huge bedrooms and 3.5 metre (11 ft, 4 in) ceilings.

Set on a quiet cul-de-sac in the suburb of Armadale minutes from the action, the cottage oozed potential with its charming period vibe. Before they knew it, Ivy and Adrian became shell-shocked homeowners, with the wheels set in motion for a large-scale project!

TIMING

Ivy and Adrian bought the Armadale house in November, 2017, finally settling the property in January, 2018. Once they'd moved in, it took Ivy nearly a year to finalise the design documentation, receive the necessary permits from her local municipality and collate the information needed to engage a builder. She used this time to collect design inspiration for the interior design and to source the right finishes, fittings and appliances for their new home. She says of the process, 'I had hoped it would only take six months, but in hindsight I should have started the moment we won the auction in 2017!' Construction of the extension started in April, 2019 with everything completed by December, 2019, a testament to Ivy's organisational skills.

VISION

Ivy wanted to create a space for her family that felt like they were always on holiday, envisioning restful, escapist bedroom suites, with an elevated central space for all to share and enjoy. 'For the façade, I wanted to maintain the cottage look, but internally I wanted to avoid something overly traditional. We're in central Melbourne, so I wanted it to feel like the city – a balance between mod cons and heritage.

'I wanted to respect the origins of the house without being historically obsessed. I also love entertaining and we receive visitors often, so we really focused on creating sanctuary-like spaces for bedrooms and bathrooms, and large, shared living areas with an emphasis on natural light and greenery, leveraging every opportunity for indoor–outdoor spaces.'

1.   A new colour scheme for a period front door can give a home's exterior a wonderful lift.

2.   Ivy added a pop of colour to this mirror to add an element of fun to her *en suite*.

3.   It can be hard to make generous-sized bedrooms feel cosy. Ivy added heavy curtains and a variety of textures and soft fabrics to help with this.

Over the page. A high-raked ceiling with exposed rafters adds volume and drama to the space. The kitchen and dining area is an entertainer's paradise, opening up with large sliding doors to the back garden.

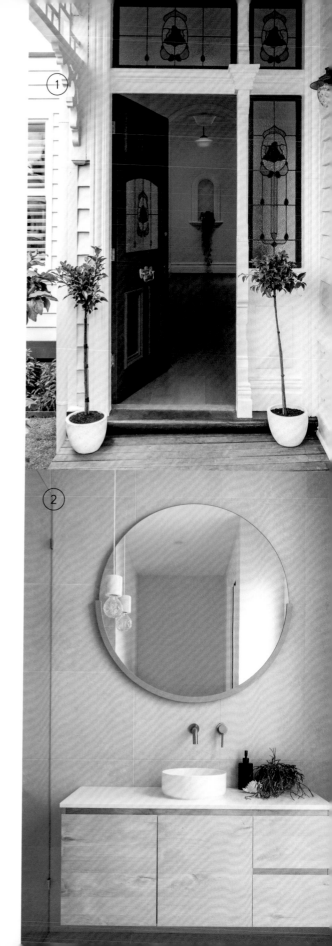

CHALLENGES !

As this was Ivy's first project, the speed bumps came hard and fast. Ivy has considerable experience in heavy industry, having previously worked on mining sites in Tanzania, yet she quickly realised the false sense of confidence this had instilled.

Ivy found BuildHer as she was struggling with site communication, encountering dishonest and condescending trades who showed frustration with, she believes, her age, gender and lack of experience. Ivy's objective had been to learn as much as possible on site, yet when the trades don't want to speak to you, this becomes near impossible.

Not having enough knowledge to know if trades were being honest, and finding that many of her team directed communication towards her partner when he was around (despite it being Ivy's project to control), Ivy was keen to improve her knowledge – and fast.

One of the first hurdles the couple experienced was hiring a dishonest tradesperson who they quickly realised was set to rip them off. Battling feelings of hopelessness in the face of this conman, they decided not to let him get away with it. Putting him under pressure, the couple created a situation where he could not achieve his unethical objective, and thus ended the relationship. Overcoming this first hurdle gave Ivy great confidence to take control of her trades.

RESULT

Although Ivy and Adrian admit that they were largely unprepared and naïve about the huge project ahead of them, the striking results of their tiresome efforts truly speak for themselves: a four-bedroom, single-storey Edwardian weatherboard home with contemporary extensions on a block just shy of 400 m² (4300 ft²). 'Three of the bedrooms were designed to feel like sanctuaries, each offering the privacy of an *en suite* bathroom. The fourth bedroom doubles as a second living area, depending on how many guests are staying, which opens onto a courtyard via large glass sliding doors. Ivy's decision to add wall panelling and white sheers provide another level of decadence and romance to this flexible space.

'We added a hallway arch, which resonates with the original niche in the entry hallway. There is also a ceiling rose and large cornices in each room, even in the main bathroom. Conveniently, darker floorboards are quite Edwardian, as well as current, so we kept those. We also restored the cast-iron fireplaces to their original glory.

'At the rear, we built a spacious open-plan kitchen–living room with a cathedral ceiling. Walking in, your eyes are immediately drawn upwards and it's a "wow" moment. One side of the room is entirely glass, which opens up onto the lush backyard.'

The weatherboard panelling so worthy of restoration also had to be largely replaced with fire-proof cement boarding, creating a modern aesthetic in keeping with the original exterior.

Completing her vision with polish, Ivy worked closely with a kitchen designer over 10 iterations to nail the final look. Luxe cabinetry wraps around a huge island bar topped with Carrara marble, a finish that carries through to the splash back and into numerous wet areas, including the polished marble tiles in the main bathroom. Ivy says, 'I chose all the finishes myself. Because it was my first project, I played it a little safe, sticking to more classic finishes rather than trends. Maybe in the future I'd take more risks.'

1–2. In the kitchen, Ivy paired marble with dark contrasting timber cabinets and gold taps.

3.   The living space features highlight windows, a modern fireplace, built-in joinery and a sofa.

4.   This room, with its own private outdoor coutryard, is painted in neutral tones to allow future owners to put their mark on this flexible space.

5.   Indoor–outdoor living is a must in Melbourne. Ivy installed large sliding doors to create a 4 metre (13 ft) opening, which gives a fabulous connection to the back garden.

TIPS

It wasn't until the framing stage of the build that Ivy discovered BuildHer. Given her time again, and now knowing what she knows from experience, she says she would start planning a property's design before purchasing. As it was, with the framework in place, Rebeka came to visit the site and Ivy subsequently made the most of the BuildHer Facebook community. This support network helped her to take control of the second phase of the building process.

Ivy's top tip for inexperienced project managers is to find that support network. 'There's nothing that builds confidence quite like the support and encouragement of a community of women working through the same process!'

This support network also extends to reliable trades. After their initial experience with a bad trade, Ivy sourced properly verified recommendations for the rest of the build, and can't speak highly enough of the difference this made to her project, both for her first project management experience, and to the final result.

Finally, Ivy stresses the importance of nailing the design early on. 'In the future, my goal will be to lock in as much of the detail as possible before even breaking ground.'

1.   French doors and a free-standing bath give this family bathroom a sense of elegance, while the curtains add a softness to hard surfaces.

2–3. Ivy used English tap wear throughout the property.

4.   A free-standing vanity unit in black ties the room together.

When Ivy began the project, the plan was never to sell. But after tough initial hurdles, Ivy loved the process so much that she's made the big decision to take up development full time. Ivy's next step was to complete the BuildHer masterclass to learn about developing property, and she has already bought another renovator's delight.

For her second project, Ivy says she plans to execute her build in a more informed order – making better initial decisions before finding herself in at the deep end. The Armadale auction couldn't have been timed better, with four bidders battling it out and the property selling for well above the reserve price.

Ivy has also joined forces with Rebeka, Kribashini and five other BuildHers in a joint venture development project, where she is leading the PR and marketing. Despite all the challenges, Ivy has discovered a career-changing passion.

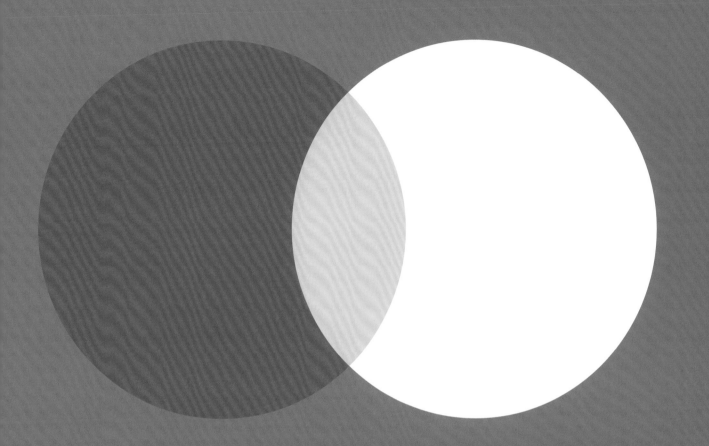

MOVING IN!

HANDOVER

The handover process happens just before you move into your new home – woohoo! This is arguably the most important stage of the entire project because it's also about acceptance. You've achieved something incredible, but the end result may or may not be exactly what you had envisioned on day one.

If you have a good relationship with your builder, the handover should be a painless process without the need for pointing fingers at mistakes made along the way. Understanding your builder's handover process is critical to know before you engage them, so do your research!

At handover, you need to keep in mind what is reasonable and what is not. The process should only start when all the building works on the drawings are finished. Some builders may try to hand over the keys while they're still on site finishing external works. This is okay if it's acceptable to you, but remember that it is not the builder's right to do this, and it should be discussed with you prior to the handover commencing.

Your builder will have completed their own inspection of your property, detailing unfinished works or defects. A building surveyor is then required to complete a final inspection. If the building surveyor is satisfied that the works comply with local building codes, they will issue a certificate of occupancy. This is a legal document that means the building is now ready to be used – hooray! It does not mean that all defects and all workmanship are perfect; that is not the job of the building surveyor.

You may choose to complete your own inspection of the building works or engage someone to do this on your behalf, such as an independent building consultant. From this inspection, there will be a defects' list from which the builder may come back to address or debate any issues. There may also be some negotiation over variations requested during the build. Once these are resolved, the builder will issue their final invoice along with all the keys to the property if you're moving into a new house. Alternatively, they may request the main contract is paid out before handing over the keys. They may provide warranties and installation guides to appliances and fixtures, along with cleaning information.

Once you move in, styling your new space is all part of the fun. Spend time placing artwork until you find the perfect spot.

SETTLING IN

As you learn to live in and love your home, be sure to note down any issues that crop up along the way. Remember that fixtures and fittings are new, so there will probably be a few teething issues over the first few months.

Common problems include doors not opening and closing perfectly, toilets backing up due to damaged pipes, adjustments to taps, problems with water pressure, catching automated garage doors or gates and occasional left-over paint spatters. Generally, these are not big problems and most builders expect to be called back a few times to make small adjustments.

On a happier note, you are now living in your brand new home! A home you dreamed of, saved for, worked really hard to create and invested many hours in time and energy. Now is the time to step back, soak it all in and reap the rewards of all your work. Take joy in noticing the little things: the way your kitchen functions and flows because you designed that way; the comfort you feel kicking back on the couch; or the luxury of your new *en suite*. You should feel proud, so make sure you celebrate your incredible achievement. Well done and enjoy the many exciting moments ahead.

Indoor plants bring life to any room. Mix and match foliage with your favourite trinkets to transform shelving into a standalone feature.

Top Tip

Did you know that in Australia there is a document called the Standards and Tolerances Guide, which states what constitutes a reasonable defect? One of the rules is that you need to stand at least 1.5 metres (4 ft, 9 in) away from a wall to pick a defect in a paint job! Find out if there is a similar guide in your country.

GLOSSARY: WHO YOU'LL MEET ALONG THE WAY

There are many individuals you may encounter throughout your building journey. Here, we give a brief overview of some of the professionals you're likely to meet and their roles.

COUNCIL

Building surveyor/Certifier: These professionals make sure that your plans comply with local building regulations. You will engage them to act on your behalf to review and approve relevant documentation, check that the property is built in accordance with the plans and then finally sign off to say that your home is finished and habitable.

Planning officer: Members of your local council or authority, planning officers review your proposed renovation or build to ensure that the design complies with any restrictions or overlays pertaining to your local area.

DESIGN

Architect: A registered professional with a post-graduate degree, qualified to take on all aspects of internal and external design.

Civil engineer: An engineer who ensures that sewerage and storm-water systems are designed correctly. Civil engineers are normally only needed for more complex builds or subdivisions.

Draftsperson: A qualified building designer who undertakes all technical drawings of a build or renovation using CAD (computer-aided design).

Geotechnical engineer: A professional who tests the soil for its bearing capacity and subsequently provides a report that the structural engineer must adhere to.

Interior designer: As the name suggests, these professionals focus on the design of interiors, including layouts, materials and furnishings.

Landscape architect: Responsible for all garden design, including hardscaping (paths, decks and driveways) and soft landscaping (plants and trees).

Structural engineer: Responsible for the structural design of a building, along with providing certification that the resulting structure can withstand live loads, such as people, furniture, winds and the weight of its own construction.

Depending on the complexity of a build, other specialists and/or engineers may be required, including services for mechanical ventilation and heating, electrical, traffic control and more.

TRADESPEOPLE

Brick layer: A brick and block layer can build masonry walls, retaining walls, brick fencing and double-skinned or single-skinned brick walls.

Builder: A registered builder is qualified to manage all aspects of your build. They can be contracted to manage some or all of the tradespeople required for renovation, and can procure materials on your behalf within a fixed period and price.

Carpenter: A qualified or apprentice carpenter is responsible for building your timber frame or structure. They are also responsible for indoor carpentry, such as hanging doors and fixing timbers, which include skirting boards and architraves etc. They can double as a leading hand, working as a point of contact when you can't be on site.

Carpet layer: Responsible for laying carpets or installing flooring such as timber floors.

Caulker: In some countries, caulking is a trade in itself. It is essentially someone who seals ceiling edges with waterproof caulk.

Concreter: A professional who can order and organise delivery of your concrete. They can also lay concrete foundations, paving and any other areas which require concrete, such as your driveway.

Electrician: An electrician is able to wire your lighting, power points, air conditioning and electric oven if you have one. It is important to use a suitably experienced electrician for your projects.

Excavator: A machine operator who will move soil or spoil from your site and can operate different machinery. You may be charged for the machine as well as the operator.

Glazier: Responsible for fixing and fitting glass windows and frames, glaziers are usually affiliated with a window or door supplier. They can work with aluminium, steel or timber windowframes, but bear in mind that materials often come from different suppliers.

Joiner: Responsible for supplying and installing customised joinery, such as kitchen cabinetry, vanities or wardrobes according to specific plans.

Painter: Responsible for external and internal painting, including the preparation of surfaces, such as sanding and filling.

Plasterer: An individual who can hang dry walls or plasterboard onto your timber frame. They can often install cornicing as well.

Plumbers: A sanitary plumber will plumb your hot and cold water and sewerage, connecting your toilet and shower drains. Roof plumbers lay roofing sheets, gutters and storm-water connections. Gas plumbers connect your gas stove, hot water and heating system. Try and find a plumber who can take on all of these roles; otherwise you may need two or three plumbers on the job.

Steel fabricator: A person who draws, fabricates and installs steel structures. Depending on the individual, they may also create custom-made steel frames for mounting materials.

Tiler: A tiling professional doesn't need to be licensed; however, you want to make sure they are able to complete your project with good workmanship. They can waterproof as well as tile wet areas, floors and walls. They will sometimes provide caulking as well. You may choose to buy your own tiles, or ask your tiler to purchase tiles on your behalf. Make sure your tiler is responsible for grout and tools!

THANKS

We would like to thank our BuildHers and DevelopHers who inspire us every day with their achievements and amazing dedication. Thank you also to our professional friends near and far who support us, our community and what we do!

I would like to give special thanks to Cian, my husband, who is my biggest supporter and sounding board; my family, who are always there to help when I need them or ask; my brother, who moved in for three months to help us with our renovation at the drop of a hat; my dad, who is always ready to tackle a job on the 'to do' list; and my mum and sister, who are always ready to lend a hand when I ask. Finally, thanks to my niece Anika who transcribed my initial verbal draft!

I never in a million years thought I would write a book but here I am. In my career I've been lucky to have worked with and been mentored by some of the best people I know. People who were willing to teach me what they knew and encourage me to take on harder and more complex projects, always pushing me to do better. I am even luckier that those colleagues have turned into true friends.

I get to have the best job now, helping women build the homes or developments they dream of, while doing my bit to encourage them into an industry that is unique and exciting, and where you get to leave your mark on the world.

Lastly, Rebeka, you are the only person I would be with on this wild ride!

Kribashini Xx

There are some truly wonderful and supportive people in my life and unfortunately the list is too long to thank everyone individually. Building houses is a team sport! Each player has their role and their contribution is appreciated.

A massive and special thank you to John, my partner in life and in building. Every decision we make we make together and without you there would be no book because there would be no houses. The kids – Liam, Ben, Emily, Jack, Bear, Kitty and Tadhg – have made this incredible journey with us, living in many of our builds and renovations, spending weekends on bobcats, moving furniture and creating dream homes alongside us.

To my mum and dad, Helen and Mick, and sister, Caity, thank you for your constant support, talking through the builds, lending, selecting and moving furniture, looking at the finances and being there every step of the way. An extra special thanks to my mum, who has grafted in so many ways, and notably helped us plant out each of the gardens.

Finally, thank you so much to Alex, who has been my constant guide, and Kribashini, yes, this is one wild ride and I am so grateful I get to ride alongside you.

Rebeka Xx

We would both like to shout out and say thank you to these lovely people for all their help putting this book together: John from Beirin Projects, Jacqueline Alanne, Dylan James, Alison Lewis, Stephanie O'Sullivan, Samantha Sutton, Caitlin Jageurs (Byrnes), Maddie Witter, Ivy Huang; and our wonderful team at BuildHer Collective Headquarters, a group of truly inspirational women, who help others build every day. A special thanks to Lisa – no words can explain our immense gratitude for the role you play – Tamara, our rock, and Rachel, our shooting star!

Building is always a team effort and so many hands, brains and ideas form the final product that you see. We are forever grateful to the people we work with in this industry. Special shout-outs go to: Justine Murphy, Melissa Bailey, Sarah Minson, Steph Pirovano, Emma O'Meara and Bellemo & Cat for their work on Cunningham, Bayview and James Street, and Ardent Architects for their work on Naroon Road, all of which are featured in this book. A massive thanks to Sam Rigopoulos from Jellis Craig Real Estate who has been incredibly generous with his knowledge, time and support!

Finally, we would like to thank our publisher Paul McNally for believing in us and what we stand for, our editors Lucy Heaver and Hannah Koelmeyer who have made writing this book a joy, and our amazing designer Michelle Mackintosh for her gorgeous design work.

Published in 2021 by Smith Street Books
Naarm | Melbourne | Australia
smithstreetbooks.com

Hardcover ISBN: 978-1-922417-01-5
Flexi-bound ISBN: 978-1-922417-40-4

Publisher: Lucy Heaver, Tusk studio
Commissioned by: Hannah Koelmeyer
Editor: Lucy Heaver, Tusk studio
Designer: Michelle Mackintosh
Cover design: Michelle Mackintosh
Layout: Megan Ellis
Photography: Dylan James and Martina Gemmola (for Haymes Paint)

Personal artwork featured in this book: 'Dreaming is Free' by Charlie
Macrae and 'Blueberry Afternoon' by Marika Borlase (Forman
Framing); 'Bearded Iris & Dogwood' by Samantha Michelle; 'Emu
Dreaming' by Lee Nangala Gallagher (Art Ark); 'Integrated' and 'Love
Your Way' by Sarah Kelk; 'Black Betty' by Amelia Anderson; 'Pretzel'
by Rachel Castle; Brigitte Bardot (from Schots Home Emporium);
artwork (on desk) by Stacey Rees; 'Highways' by John Trif; 'Rain' by
Katie Wyatt.

Printed & bound in China by C&C Offset Printing Co., Ltd.

Book 160
10 9 8 7 6 5 4 3 2 1